Reading Voyage

1

BASIC

BASIC 1

Publisher Chung Kyudo
Editors Jeong Yeonsoon, Kim Mina
Authors Milton Prep, Jonathan S. McClelland, Brian Stuart
Proofreader Jonathan S. McClelland
Designer Design Sum

First published in May 2016
By Darakwon, Inc.
Darakwon Bldg., 211, Munbal-ro, Paju-si, Gyeonggi-do 10881
Republic of Korea
Tel: 82-2-736-2031 (Ext. 250)
Fax: 82-2-732-2037

Copyright © 2016 Darakwon, Inc.

All rights reserved. No part of this publication may be reproduced, stored in a retrieval system, or transmitted in any form or by any means, electronic, mechanical, photocopying or otherwise, without the prior consent of the copyright owner. Refund after purchase is possible only according to the company regulations. Contact the above telephone number for any inquiries. Consumer damages caused by loss, damage, etc. can be compensated according to the consumer dispute resolution standards announced by the Korea Fair Trade Commission. An incorrectly collated book will be exchanged.

ISBN 978-89-277-5198-4 58740
       978-89-277-0773-8 58740 (set)

www.darakwon.co.kr

Components Main Book / Workbook
15 14 13 12 11 10 9   25 26 27 28 29

Reading
Voyage

BASIC

1

Unit Components

Before You Read

This section helps students make predictions about the topic by drawing on their background knowledge before reading the passage.

Students can preview the key vocabulary words by checking the ones that they already know.

Main Reading Passage

A focus sentence before each passage gives students tips to help them understand the main idea of the text.

The passages are written to be as interesting and informative as possible, covering a variety of topics. In addition to standard articles, passage formats include short essays, letters, and interviews. This variety of styles helps students become accustomed to reading various types of English texts.

Vocabulary in Context

This section helps students learn the key words from the passage by matching the words with their definitions.

Reading Comprehension

This portion asks students to identify the main idea, details, and draw inferences from the passages through multiple-choice and short-answer questions.

Reading Skill

Students can organize the key concepts of the passage by practicing various reading skills including identifying the main idea, sequencing, cause and effect, and more.

Summary

Students can review the essential information from the passage through the summary.

Vocabulary Expansion

This section presents synonyms, antonyms, prefixes, and suffixes for the key vocabulary words, helping students to expand their vocabularies.

Students can review the key words from the passage in different contexts by completing the sentences.

Workbook   Extra vocabulary and writing practice are provided to enable students to understand the material more deeply.

Online Supplement   MP3 files, answer keys, translations, and vocabulary lists are provided free online at www.darakwon.co.kr. A program for generating vocabulary and writing test sheets is available free online at voca.darakwon.co.kr.

Table of Contents

Unit	Theme	Title	Reading Skill	Page
1	Food	**A Delicious British Food**	Sequencing	9
2	Jobs	**Repairing a Signal Tower**	Main Idea & Details	13
3	Language	**What Does It Mean?**	Main Idea & Details	17
4	Origins	**What Is Black Friday?**	Main Idea	21
5	Health	**I Cannot Eat Peanut Butter!**	Cause & Effect	25
6	Psychology	**The Story of Narcissus**	Sequencing	29
7	Places	**The Hottest Place in the World**	Main Idea & Details	33
8	People	**Andy Goldsworthy, a Unique Artist**	Main Idea & Details	37
9	Sociology	**City, Town, Village**	Compare & Contrast	41
10	History	**Starbucks of the 18th Century**	Categorizing	45

Unit	Theme	Title	Reading Skill	Page
11	Environment	**Why Trees Matter**	Main Idea & Details	49
12	Social Issues	**Penny Harvest**	Sequencing	53
13	Daily Life	**Tips for Saving Time**	Cause & Effect	57
14	Mysteries	**The Amber Room**	Sequencing	61
15	Astronomy	**Where Did the Moon Come from?**	Categorizing	65
16	Technology	**The Mysterious Box on Airplanes**	Cause & Effect	69
17	Nature	**Wasps Help Protect Corn**	Sequencing	73
18	Sports	**Weird Sports**	Categorizing	77
19	Technology	**The Future of Travel**	Categorizing	81
20	People	**The Power of a Dream**	Sequencing	85

Theme | *Food*
Reading Skill | *Sequencing*

Unit 1

A Delicious British Food

◀ Cottage pie

Before You Read

A What do you know about cottage pie? Check *T* or *F*.

1. Cottage pie is a new dish.   T / F
2. Cottage pie comes from Britain.   T / F
3. Cottage pie is usually made with sugar and fruit.   T / F

B Look at the vocabulary and check the ones you know.

☐ fancy   ☐ brown   ☐ cuisine

☐ mash   ☐ simmer   ☐ ingredient

A Delicious British Food

▶ *As you read, focus on how to make cottage pie.*

Britain is famous for its meat pies. And cottage pie, or shepherd's pie, is the most famous of them all. It's not really a "pie" because it's not made with pastry. It's made with **mashed** potatoes.

Cottage pie has been a part of British culture and **cuisine** for hundreds of years. But it was never meant to be a **fancy** meal. It was just a way that families could use up their leftover meat and potatoes. And it's really quite easy to make. All you need are a few simple ingredients.

First, **brown** about 1 kilogram of ground beef. Add chopped carrots, celery, and onions to the pan and fry them for about 5 minutes. Add the beef back to the pan and pour in beef stock. **Simmer** everything and cook for 45 minutes. While you are cooking this, boil some potatoes until they are soft and mash them with milk, butter, and cheddar cheese. Put the meat in a pan and spread the mashed potatoes on top. Then slide it into the oven and bake it at 200 degrees Celsius for 25-30 minutes.

It's a very easy and delicious meal that anyone can make. You should try it!

Words 199

Vocabulary in Context
Write the words in bold next to their correct definitions.

1. _____ to cook on low heat
2. _____ to make brown by cooking
3. _____ to crush food into a soft mass
4. _____ high in quality; not plain or ordinary
5. _____ food that is cooked in a particular way

Reading Comprehension

1 **What is this passage mainly about?**

a. a famous British chef
b. a typical British food
c. British cooking class
d. the history of British cuisine

2 **Why did British people invent cottage pie?**

_____

3 **Which is NOT true about cottage pie?**

a. It is easy to make.
b. It is a recent British dish.
c. It is a famous dish in Britain.
d. It is made with beef and potatoes.

4 **What is NOT mentioned as ingredients in cottage pie?**

a. chopped garlic
b. ground beef
c. chopped carrots
d. mashed potatoes

5 **According to the passage, what can you guess about cottage pie?**

a. It costs a lot of money to make.
b. All ingredients should be ground.
c. It takes more than an hour to make.
d. It is unpopular among British people.

Reading Skill *Sequencing is putting events in order from first to last. When we sequence, we can easily understand which events happen first, second, and so on.*

Fill in the chart and number the steps for making cottage pie in order.

❶_____ 1 kilogram of ground beef.
❷_____ at 200 degrees Celsius for 25-30 minutes.
Boil and ❸_____ potatoes with cheese, milk, and butter.
Put the meat in a pan and put the potatoes on ❹_____.
Fry the vegetables and ❺_____ the beef and vegetables in beef stock.

mash   brown   bake   simmer   top

Summary

Use the words in the box to complete the summary.

brown	fancy	cuisine	simmer	ground

Cottage pie is a famous dish in British ①_____. Its main ingredients are ②_____ beef, mashed potatoes, milk, butter, cheese, and vegetables. To make it, first ③_____ the beef. Then fry the vegetables and ④_____ everything in beef stock. Then mash the potatoes and put them on top of the meat. After that, bake everything for 25-30 minutes. It's not a ⑤_____ meal, but it's delicious!

Vocabulary Expansion

A   Match the words with their similar meanings from the box.

remaining	high-quality	consume

Words	Similar Meaning
fancy	_____
use up	_____
leftover	_____

B   Fill in the blanks using the words in bold from the passage. Change the forms if necessary.

1. Use a fork to _____ the strawberries in the bowl.
2. Put the soup on low heat and let it _____ for 30 minutes.
3. _____ the beef in a frying pan, but don't cook it all the way.
4. Indian food is one of the most popular types of _____ in the world.
5. I don't like to wear _____ clothes. I just like to wear jeans and a T-shirt.

Theme | *Jobs*
Reading Skill | *Main Idea & Details*

Unit 2

Repairing a Signal Tower

Before You Read

A What do you know about signal towers? Check *T* or *F*.

1. Signal towers are very tall.   T / F
2. Signal towers are easy to fix.   T / F
3. Nobody climbs up signal towers.   T / F

B Look at the vocabulary and check the ones you know.

☐ repair   ☐ pole   ☐ train
☐ harness   ☐ technician   ☐ uncomfortable

Repairing a Signal Tower

▶ *As you read, focus on how technicians climb signal towers to fix them.*

*Signal towers can be very tall. Some of them are taller than the Empire State Building. The tallest ones are nearly 540 meters tall! Sometimes these towers need to be **repaired**. That means **technicians** must climb to the top of these towers. How do the technicians do this?

It's a long climb to the top. First, they take an elevator to about 490 meters. Then, the technicians have to get out of the elevator and start climbing. They use a safety belt to climb. The very top part is the scariest of all. Here, there is only a thin **pole** with large bolts in it. The technicians must climb these bolts for 30 more meters. At the top of the pole, technicians have to work fast. If a storm comes, there is no quick way down, except to fall!

Repairing a signal tower may look like a dangerous job, but the technicians are well **trained**. They quickly get used to climbing to the top of the tower. Many don't even use safety **harnesses** while they climb, and accidents are really quite rare. Still, climbing a 540-meter tower is an uncomfortable way to spend your working day. **Words 196**

*signal tower: a tall structure that sends out radio or television signals

Vocabulary in Context

Write the words in bold next to their correct definitions.

1. _____ to fix
2. _____ a long, thin piece of wood or metal
3. _____ to teach someone how to do something
4. _____ a person who is trained to fix machines or computers
5. _____ pieces of material put around the shoulders to keep a person from falling

Reading Comprehension

1 What is the main idea of this passage?

a. Repairing a signal tower is a scary job.
b. Signal towers often need to be repaired.
c. Technicians are well trained to do difficult work.
d. Wearing the proper safety equipment is very important.

2 What do technicians do first when they repair a signal tower?

_____

3 What do technicians NOT use to go up a signal tower?

a. a thin pole
b. a staircase
c. an elevator
d. a safety belt

4 Which is true about signal tower technicians?

a. They work slowly.
b. They have many accidents.
c. They get lots of training.
d. They repair safety harnesses.

5 According to the passage, what can you guess about signal towers?

a. They break every day.
b. They are easy to repair.
c. It is very dangerous to repair them in bad weather.
d. A lot of technicians have been injured repairing them.

Reading Skill *The main idea is usually at the beginning of a text and makes a general statement. The supporting details are specific ideas that support the main idea.*

Fill in the chart with the words in the box.

Paragraph 1	Technicians must ❶_____ signal towers. • Technicians must ❷_____ to the top of these towers.
Paragraph 2	It's a long climb to the top of a signal tower. • Technicians take ❸_____ and climb a 30-meter pole.
Paragraph 3	Technicians are ❹_____ for a long time to do this job. • ❺_____ do not happen often.

trained　　repair　　accidents　　climb　　the elevator

Summary

Use the words in the box to complete the summary.

wrong   pole   safety   trained   signal tower

Climbing a ❶_____ is a dangerous and scary job. Signal towers are extremely tall. Sometimes something goes ❷_____ and they need to be repaired. The only way to do that is to climb them—even the tall, thin ❸_____ at the top. Technicians are well ❹_____ and skilled workers. They climb these tall towers without fear, and often without the proper ❺_____ equipment: harnesses.

Vocabulary Expansion

A **Match the words with their similar meanings from the box.**

fix   almost   mount

Words	Similar Meaning
climb	_____
repair	_____
nearly	_____

B **Fill in the blanks using the words in bold from the passage. Change the forms if necessary.**

1. A flag is usually put at the top of a tall _____.
2. You should call a _____ to fix this equipment.
3. The storm hit our garage, but it was _____ in a week.
4. You need to wear a _____ when you learn rock-climbing.
5. Firefighters are _____ to put out fires and save people's lives.

Theme | *Language*
Reading Skill | *Main Idea & Details*

Unit 3

What Does It Mean?

Before You Read

A Do you use Internet slang? Take this writing habits quiz to find out.

1. Do you sometimes mix words together or make them shorter?
2. Do you take a lot of time to write messages with good spelling and grammar?
3. Do you have trouble understanding messages if somebody does not spell words normally?

B Look at the vocabulary and check the ones you know.

☐ confuse   ☐ humble   ☐ substitute
☐ delete   ☐ slang   ☐ common

What Does It Mean?

▶ As you read, try to guess the meanings of the slang words before reading the definitions.

Dear Karen,
   Your email had some strange words. You wrote "IMHO" to begin a sentence. At the end, you wrote "Cya." What do these mean?
Thanks,
Charlie

Hi Charlie,
   I'm sorry to **confuse** you with Internet **slang**. I use it to type faster. There are two main types of Internet slang: acronyms and abbreviations. Acronyms use the first letter of each word in a phrase. For example, "IMHO" means "in my **humble** opinion." An abbreviation is when you delete the less important letters in a word. For example, "ATTN" is a shorter way of typing "attention."
   Sometimes, people **substitute** numbers or letters that sound like words. "Cya" is an abbreviation of "See you later!" In this case, the letter "c" sounds like "see." Another one is "gr8." Can you guess what it means? Great! Some **common** Internet slang words are: BRB = be right back, BTW = by the way, and L8TR = later. There are also hundreds of symbols called emoticons. You must have seen them before: :-) = "I'm smiling." It's fun to use these with friends.
Cya!
Karen   Words 181

Vocabulary in Context
Write the words in bold next to their correct definitions.

1. _____ modest
2. _____ often used
3. _____ casual or playful words
4. _____ to use someone or something in place of another
5. _____ to make someone unable to understand something

Reading Comprehension

1 **What is the main idea of the emails?**

    a. Internet slang should not be used.

    b. Everyone easily understands Internet slang.

    c. Internet slang has several different forms.

    d. You can buy a dictionary about Internet slang.

2 **Which letters of each word are used to make an acronym?**

    a. the most important letters   b. the first letters

    c. only the first and last letters   d. the last letters

3 **What is "Cya" an abbreviation for?**

_____

4 **Which is NOT true according to the passage?**

    a. "ATTN" is an acronym for attention.

    b. An emoticon shows how someone is feeling.

    c. You can type faster by using Internet slang.

    d. An abbreviation eliminates the least important letters in a word.

5 **According to the emails, you can guess that ASAP is an _____ for as soon as possible.**

    a. ending   b. acronym

    c. abbreviation   d. emoticon

Reading Skill

The main idea makes a general statement. The supporting details are specific ideas that support the main idea.

Fill in the chart with the words in the box.

Main Idea	People use many ❶_____ forms of Internet slang.
Details	• Acronyms use only the ❷_____ of each word in a phrase. • Abbreviations ❸_____ the less important letters in a word. • People also use ❹_____. These are little ❺_____ that show how a person feels.

    delete   symbols   emoticons   different   first letter

Summary

Use the words in the box to complete the summary.

emoticons   abbreviations   feeling   confusing   acronyms

Internet slang can be ❶_____ to people at first, but it is not hard to figure out. Basically, there are three types of Internet slang. First, there are ❷_____. These are formed by the first letter of each word in a phrase. Second, there are ❸_____. These are formed by taking out the less important letters in a word. Finally, there are ❹_____, which are little symbols that show how a person is ❺_____.

Vocabulary Expansion

A Match the words with their similar and opposite meanings from the box.

add   rare   modest   remove   arrogant   typical

Words	Similar Meaning	Opposite Meaning
humble	_____	_____
delete	_____	_____
common	_____	_____

B Fill in the blanks using the words in bold from the passage. Change the forms if necessary.

1. It's okay to use _____ with your friends.
2. Electric door locks are _____ in South Korean homes.
3. Jake pretends to be _____, but he is actually arrogant.
4. These directions _____ me. I can't figure out what they mean.
5. Mr. Brown is going to _____ for our regular teacher while he is on vacation.

Theme | *Origins*
Reading Skill | *Main Idea*

Unit 4

What Is Black Friday?

Before You Read

A Are you a compulsive shopper? Take this shopping habits quiz to find out.

1. Do you shop just to make yourself feel good?
2. Do you shop when you feel stressed?
3. Do you buy clothes that you never wear?

B Look at the vocabulary and check the ones you know.

- ☐ term
- ☐ rush
- ☐ take place
- ☐ attract
- ☐ employer
- ☐ day off

What Is Black Friday?

▶ *As you read, focus on how Black Friday came to be.*

Every Black Friday, shopping malls and department stores have giant sales. People **rush** to get toys and other products at the cheapest prices all year. Sometimes people even get injured in the big, excited crowds at the malls. Black Friday is the biggest shopping day in the United States.

Black Friday **takes place** on the day after Thanksgiving in the U.S. Usually, employers give their employees the **day off**. This makes it a good day to go shopping. So malls and stores started offering big sales on that day. They also stay open later than usual on Black Friday.

People started calling the day after Thanksgiving "Black Friday" in the 1950s. Police called it "Black Friday" because of heavy traffic and big crowds. Magazines and newspapers started calling it Black Friday too.

Soon, everyone was using the **term**. Stores started having sales to **attract** customers. And now, Black Friday means a day for shopping. If you go to the U.S. for Thanksgiving, buy a present on Black Friday. Just don't get hurt in the crowds!

Words 175

Vocabulary in Context

Write the words and phrases in bold next to their correct definitions.

1. _____ to happen
2. _____ to move or go quickly
3. _____ to cause to come to a place
4. _____ a day when you do not have to work
5. _____ a word or phrase to describe something

Reading Comprehension

1 **What is the best title for this passage?**

a. An Event in U.S. History
b. Thanksgiving in the 1950s
c. A Popular Festival in the U.S.
d. A Popular Day for Shopping

2 **When is Black Friday?**

a. the last day of the year
b. the day after Thanksgiving
c. the day before Thanksgiving
d. the day of Thanksgiving

3 **Why is Black Friday a good shopping day?**

a. The stores open early that day.
b. There is very little traffic that day.
c. Many employees have that day off.
d. Most stores have more items that day.

4 **Why did police call the day "Black Friday" in the 1950s?**

_____

5 **According to the passage, what can you guess about Black Friday?**

a. It lasts for at least three days.
b. Many people shop on that day.
c. It is the most relaxing day for shopping.
d. There are several Black Fridays after other holidays.

Reading Skill *In most paragraphs, the main idea is usually the first sentence. It gives a general idea that is explained in the rest of the paragraph.*

Fill in the chart with the words in the box.

Paragraph 1	Black Friday is a ❶_____ shopping day in the U.S.
Paragraph 2	Black Friday happens on the day after ❷_____.
Paragraph 3	The ❸_____ "Black Friday" started in the 1950s.
Paragraph 4	Now, Black Friday means a day for ❹_____.

shopping   term   popular   Thanksgiving

Unit 4   23

Summary

Use the words and phrases in the box to complete the summary.

day off	rush	attract	takes place	employers

Black Friday is an important shopping day in the U.S. It ❶_____ on the day after Thanksgiving. The term "Black Friday" started in the 1950s. Many ❷_____ started giving their workers the ❸_____ on Black Friday. That way, people could do a lot of shopping on that day. Stores began to have big sales on Black Friday to ❹_____ customers. Now, people ❺_____ to the stores to buy cheap goods on Black Friday.

Vocabulary Expansion

A **Match the words with their similar meanings from the box.**

hurry	provide	phrase

Words	Similar Meaning
term	_____
rush	_____
offer	_____

B **Fill in the blanks using the words and phrases in bold from the passage. Change the forms if necessary.**

1. Tomorrow night's concert _____ at Greenwood Park.
2. We had a _____ from school because of the heavy snow.
3. Action movies _____ a lot of male teenagers to the cinema.
4. You should not use _____ like "shut up" in the classroom.
5. We have to _____ to get all of our work finished before 5 o'clock.

Theme | *Health*
Reading Skill | *Cause & Effect*

Unit 5

I Cannot Eat Peanut Butter!

Before You Read

A What do you know about allergies? Check *T* or *F*.

1. They can be caused by food.   T / F
2. They're never very dangerous.   T / F
3. Doctors can test for them.   T / F

B Look at the vocabulary and check the ones you know.

☐ rash   ☐ occur   ☐ react
☐ cure   ☐ fool   ☐ nauseous

I Cannot Eat Peanut Butter!

▶ *As you read, focus on how allergies happen and what you can do about them.*

Did you ever meet someone who could not eat a chocolate cookie? Maybe you know a kid who is not allowed to touch a peanut. Or she is not allowed to drink milk. Maybe that kid is you. About one in every one hundred children has serious food allergies. It can make life quite difficult for them. If they eat a certain kind of food, like nuts or chocolate, they can get very sick.

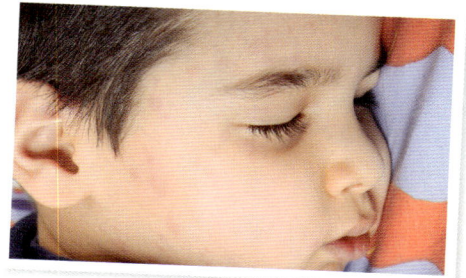

Food allergies **occur** when your body's immune system is **fooled**. Your immune system is what helps protect you from diseases. Sometimes, however, your immune system makes a mistake. It treats a harmless food like a terrible danger. Then, your body reacts very strongly to it. You may feel **nauseous** or get strong stomach pains or even have trouble breathing. You may also get **rashes** or *hives on your skin.

There is no real **cure** for allergies, so it is important to get tested for them when you are young. Doctors can find out what you are allergic to before it has a chance to make you sick.

Words 181

*hive: a raised bump on the skin

Vocabulary in Context

Write the words in bold next to their correct definitions.

1. _____ to play a trick
2. _____ to happen
3. _____ a red spot on the skin
4. _____ something that gets rid of an illness
5. _____ feeling like you want to throw up; having an upset stomach

Reading Comprehension

1 What is the main idea of this passage?

   a. Food allergies can be very dangerous.
   b. Doctors are trying to cure food allergies.
   c. Immune systems protect people from sickness.
   d. Foods that cause allergies must be kept out of schools.

2 How do food allergies occur?

   _____

3 Which is true about food allergies according to the passage?

   a. They can be cured.
   b. They only affect adults.
   c. They are caused by rotten food.
   d. Chocolate and nuts can cause allergies.

4 Which is NOT mentioned as the effect of food allergies?

   a. bad headaches   b. rashes
   c. stomach pains   d. breathing trouble

5 According to the passage, what can you guess about food allergies?

   a. People who have them are not careful.
   b. The tests for them can make people sick.
   c. They do not cause serious symptoms in kids.
   d. The best treatment is to avoid the foods that cause allergies.

Reading Skill *Cause and effect is when one event causes something to happen. The cause explains why something happens, and the effect is what happens as a result.*

Fill in the chart with the words in the box.

Cause	Effect
Our ❶_____ is fooled and our body reacts ❷_____ to a harmless food.	• feel ❸_____ or get strong stomach pains • have trouble ❹_____ • get rashes or hives on your ❺_____

   skin   strongly   nauseous   breathing   immune system

Summary

Use the words in the box to complete the summary.

avoid	cure	nauseous	fooled	rashes

Food allergies occur when your body's immune system is ❶_____.
Food allergies can make you feel ❷_____, give you red ❸_____ or hives, and make you very sick. Doctors still don't have any ❹_____ for allergies, so you must be careful. You should check with the doctor to see if you have any food allergies. Then you will know which foods to ❺_____.

Vocabulary Expansion

A Match the words with their similar meanings from the box.

cheat	happen	treatment

Words	Similar Meaning
occur	_____
fool	_____
cure	_____

B Fill in the blanks using the words in bold from the passage. Change the forms if necessary.

1. There is still no _____ for colds and flus.
2. I feel _____ when I eat too much candy.
3. When I touched that plant, I got a terrible _____.
4. The magic trick _____ all of the children watching.
5. Last year, the worst snowstorm in history _____ in Canada.

Theme | *Psychology*
Reading Skill | *Sequencing*

Unit 6

The Story of Narcissus

Before You Read

A Check the statements that are true about you.

☐ 1. I look at myself in the mirror several times a day.
☐ 2. I like to take pictures of myself with my phone.
☐ 3. I think it is important to look good for other people.

B Look at the vocabulary and check the ones you know.

☐ reject   ☐ spring   ☐ reflection
☐ delight   ☐ legend   ☐ stumble across

The Story of Narcissus

▸ *As you read, focus on what caused Narcissus to fall in love.*

Dear Jane,

I got upset today. I spend a lot of time looking in a mirror, so my brother said I was a narcissist. I didn't know what that meant, so I looked it up on the Internet. I found an interesting story.

A narcissist is someone who is in love with his or her own beauty. The name comes from a Greek **legend** about a young boy named Narcissus. He was good-looking and charming. Many young women fell in love with him. Narcissus **rejected** all of them. One day, while he was hunting, he **stumbled across** a spring. Narcissus could see his **reflection** in the water. He had never seen it before. For the first time in his life, he fell in love. Narcissus just remained by the water's edge, staring in **delight** at his own image. He didn't leave, not even to eat. Finally, he grew skinny and died of hunger.

I don't think I'm like Narcissus. Sure, I like to look at myself in the mirror. But that's just to make sure I don't look silly. I don't want others to see me with messy hair or a dirty face!

Bye now,
Karen   Words 196

Vocabulary in Context

Write the words and phrases in bold next to their correct definitions.

1. _____ to refuse
2. _____ an old story; a myth
3. _____ to discover by accident
4. _____ a feeling of great happiness
5. _____ an image seen in a mirror or a shiny surface

Reading Comprehension

1 **What is this passage mainly about?**

a. what a narcissist is
b. a girl who argues with her brother
c. why teenagers like looking in mirrors
d. a boy who falls in love with his appearance

2 **What did Narcissus find while he was hunting?**

a. food
b. a mirror
c. a woman
d. a spring

3 **How did Narcissus die?**

_____

4 **Which is true according to the passage?**

a. Karen thinks she is like Narcissus.
b. At first, Karen did not know what a narcissist is.
c. Karen looks in the mirror to make sure her clothes are neat.
d. Narcissus always looked into mirrors when he was young.

5 **According to the passage, you can guess that _____.**

a. mirrors were not common in ancient Greece
b. Narcissus liked to meet his many girlfriends
c. this was the first time Narcissus went hunting
d. the word "narcissist" comes from a theory about psychology

---

Reading Skill *Sequencing is putting events in order from first to last. When we sequence, we can easily understand which events happen first, second, and so on.*

Fill in the chart and number the events in order.

He ❶_____ in love with his own image.	
He saw his ❷_____ for the first time.	
He never left the spring and died of ❸_____.	
Narcissus was hunting when he ❹_____ a spring.	

reflection   fell   hunger   stumbled across

Summary

Use the words in the box to complete the summary.

image   legend   hunger   handsome   meant

Karen's brother called her a narcissist. Karen didn't know what this word ❶_____, but she found out by reading an ancient Greek ❷_____. Narcissus was a very ❸_____ young boy who rejected many women. One day, while hunting, he saw his own ❹_____ for the first time in a spring. He fell in love with his image and died of ❺_____ because he did not want to leave his reflection. The word "narcissist" comes from his story.

Vocabulary Expansion

A The suffix "-tion" is used to make some verbs into nouns. If the verb ends in "-t", add only "-ion." Change the verbs into nouns by adding "-ion" and match each word to a definition in the chart.

reflect   educate   suggest

Words	Definition
_____	an idea about how someone should behave
_____	the action of teaching someone in a school
_____	the picture seen in a mirror or other shiny surface

B Fill in the blanks using the words and phrases in bold from the passage. Change the forms if necessary.

1. I was filled with _____ when I got my birthday gifts.

2. Some people believe in the _____ about the ghosts.

3. I _____ some interesting facts about elephants online.

4. My teacher _____ my excuse for not doing my homework.

5. Dolphins are one of the few animals that can recognize their own _____.

Theme | *Places*
Reading Skill | *Main Idea & Details*

Unit 7

The Hottest Place in the World

▲ Dallol in Ethiopia

Before You Read

A What do you know about the hottest place in the world? Check *T* or *F*.

1. The hottest place in the world is in Africa.   T / F
2. The hottest place in the world is a large town.   T / F
3. There are useful things there.   T / F

B Look at the vocabulary and check the ones you know.

☐ toxic   ☐ harsh   ☐ molten
☐ annual   ☐ planet   ☐ all year round

Unit 7 33

The Hottest Place in the World

▶ *As you read, focus on how difficult it is to live in Dallol in Ethiopia.*

Have you ever heard of the region of Dallol in Ethiopia? It is one of the most unlivable places on the **planet**. It is boiling hot **all year round** there. Dallol has the highest average **annual** temperature on Earth: 35 degrees Celsius. Dallol is not only extremely hot. It is also a highly volcanic region. Rivers of **molten** rock run under the ground. Sometimes the molten rock bubbles up to the surface and forms **toxic** lakes. These lakes are impossible for anything to live in. Dallol is also known for its earthquakes. It lies on a *fault line, so earthquakes are constantly happening.

Dallol has some value, though. Americans discovered an important mineral called potash there in the late 1910s. They soon gave up the potash mines because of the harsh conditions. Now, Dallol is known for its salt mines. A few buildings still stand around Dallol, but no one really lives there. However, people ride camels to get there and use axes to chop big pieces of salt from the ground. It's a difficult way to make a living!

Words 181

◀ Salt miners

*fault line: An area where two large parts of the Earth meet. Earthquakes often happen on fault lines.

Vocabulary in Context

Write the words and phrases in bold next to their correct definitions.

1. _____ very poisonous
2. _____ happening every year
3. _____ made into liquid by heat
4. _____ from the beginning of the year to the end
5. _____ a body of rock or gas that goes around a star in space

Reading Comprehension

1 **What is this passage mainly about?**

a. a busy market town in Africa

b. the importance of salt in Africa

c. the way potash is mined and used

d. a place where the environment is extremely harsh

2 **What is under the ground at Dallol?**

_____

3 **Which is NOT true about Dallol?**

a. Earthquakes often happen.

b. People make a living with salt.

c. The lakes in the region are home to many living things.

d. The average annual temperature is the highest on Earth.

4 **Why did Americans travel to Dallol in the late 1910s?**

a. to mine salt

b. to ride camels

c. to mine potash

d. to build buildings

5 **According to the passage, what can you guess about Dallol?**

a. Winter there is long.

b. Few people live there.

c. Many plants grow there.

d. It is owned by Americans.

Reading Skill *The main idea is usually at the beginning of a text and makes a general statement. The supporting details are specific ideas that support the main idea.*

Fill in the chart with the words in the box.

Paragraph 1	Dallol is an extremely difficult place to live. • It is very ❶_____ all year round. • It is a highly ❷_____ region. • It is known for its ❸_____.
Paragraph 2	Dallol is valuable. • Americans found ❹_____ mines there in the late 1910s. • It is known for its ❺_____ mines now.

potash   volcanic   earthquakes   hot   salt

Summary

Use the words and phrases in the box to complete the summary.

| toxic | harsh | living | highest | all year round |

There are many ❶_____ environments on our planet, but Dallol may be the worst. It is extremely hot ❷_____ in Dallol: 35 degrees Celsius. This is the ❸_____ average annual temperature in the world. There are many ❹_____ lakes and earthquakes in Dallol, too. In the late 1910s, Americans discovered potash there. Now, people in Dallol mine salt to make a ❺_____.

Vocabulary Expansion

A **Match the words with their similar meanings from the box.**

| always | poisonous | each year |

Words	Similar Meaning
toxic	_____
constantly	_____
annual	_____

B **Fill in the blanks using the words and phrases in bold from the passage. Change the forms if necessary.**

1. Earth is the third _____ from the sun.
2. Saudi Arabia is hot and dry _____.
3. Those chemicals are _____. Don't drink them.
4. Sometimes a volcano erupts and _____ lava spills out of it.
5. We'll have our _____ town celebration. It's our town's 95th birthday.

Theme | *People*
Reading Skill | *Main Idea & Details*

Unit 8

Andy Goldsworthy, a Unique Artist

Before You Read

A Do you like making art? Take this quiz about art.

1. How often do you draw or paint pictures?
2. Do you ever write poems or stories?
3. Do you like making dolls or other objects?

B Look at the vocabulary and check the ones you know.

☐ spiral ☐ icicle ☐ patience
☐ smash ☐ sculpture ☐ appreciate

Andy Goldsworthy, a Unique Artist

▶ *As you read, focus on how Andy Goldsworthy makes his art masterpieces.*

▲ Wood Line by Andy Goldsworthy

Andy Goldsworthy is a Scottish artist. He doesn't use paints to make his art. He uses nature. Stones, icicles, tree branches, leaves, and many other natural objects become part of Andy's art.

For example, he may tie many colored leaves together and put them in a river. A beautiful **spiral** chain of leaves dances on the water's surface. He also **smashes** rocks together to get colored powder from them. Then he uses water to turn the powder into paint. He puts the paint in a river. The river makes beautiful swirls of color with the paint.

He also makes beautiful **sculptures** with ice. To make one, he holds icicles up to the sun. The sun melts the ice. Then, Andy holds the icicles together until they freeze into a large piece. The sculpture lasts for a few minutes. Then the warm sun melts the ice and the sculpture is gone.

Andy's art is not easy to make. It takes **patience** and care, but it is easy to understand. That makes Andy's art something that everyone can **appreciate** and enjoy.   Words 179

▲ Springtime, Ice Spiral by Andy Goldsworthy

Vocabulary in Context
Write the words in bold next to their correct definitions.

1. _____ circling around a central point
2. _____ to hit two objects together with force
3. _____ the ability to wait a long time for something
4. _____ to enjoy something because you understand it
5. _____ a piece of art made from rock, wood, or other solid material

Reading Comprehension

1 What is the main idea of this passage?

   a. Andy Goldsworthy is not a famous artist.
   b. Andy Goldsworthy makes art from nature.
   c. Andy Goldsworthy's art is fun for children.
   d. Andy Goldsworthy wants to protect nature.

2 Why does Andy smash rocks together?

   _____

3 Which is NOT mentioned as something that Andy does?

   a. He makes sculptures with icicles.
   b. He puts colored leaves in a river.
   c. He puts the rock paint in a river.
   d. He makes statues with tree branches.

4 People enjoy Andy's art because _____.

   a. his pictures are funny
   b. they like to make things too
   c. he uses animals in his art
   d. his art is simple to understand

5 According to the passage, what can you guess about Andy's art?

   a. It does not last very long.
   b. It causes a lot of pollution.
   c. Art lovers pay too much for it.
   d. Andy only works in the summertime.

Reading Skill *The main idea is usually at the beginning of a text and makes a general statement. The supporting details are specific ideas that support the main idea.*

Fill in the chart with the words in the box.

Main Idea	Andy Goldsworthy use ❶_____ objects to make art.
Details	• He ties ❷_____ together and puts them in a river. • He smashes ❸_____ to get colored powder and turns the powder into paint. Then he puts the paint in a river. • He uses icicles to make beautiful ice ❹_____.

rocks   natural   sculptures   colored leaves

Summary

Use the words in the box to complete the summary.

patience	spiral	icicles	appreciate	smashes

Andy Goldsworthy makes art from natural objects. He ties colored leaves together and puts ❶_____ chains of leaves in a river. He also ❷_____ rocks together to get colored powder out of them. Then he mixes the powder with water to make paint. He puts the paint in a river. He also melts ❸_____ in the sun, then puts them together to make a sculpture. Andy's art takes a lot of ❹_____ and care. But it is easy to understand. So most people can ❺_____ Andy's work.

Vocabulary Expansion

A   Match the words with their similar meanings from the box.

break	enjoy	tolerance

Words	Similar Meaning
smash	_____
patience	_____
appreciate	_____

B   Fill in the blanks using the words in bold from the passage. Change the forms if necessary.

1. He _____ the window with an iron bar.
2. I studied art in school, so I can _____ modern painting.
3. We climbed the _____ staircase to the second floor.
4. My friend made a beautiful _____ of a horse with wood.
5. He doesn't have much _____. He wants everything to happen quickly.

Theme | *Sociology*
Reading Skill | *Compare & Contrast*

Unit 9

City, Town, Village

Before You Read

A Check the statements that are true about you.

☐ 1. My hometown does not have a movie theater.
☐ 2. My hometown has more than a million people in it.
☐ 3. My hometown has lots of department stores and big shopping malls.

B Look at the vocabulary and check the ones you know.

☐ legal   ☐ mayor   ☐ council
☐ collection   ☐ community   ☐ incorporated

City, Town, Village

▶ As you read, focus on the differences between cities, towns, and villages.

It can be difficult to know the difference between a city, a town, and a village. When does a village become a town and a town become a city? In a way, the difference is simple.

A city is large and has many people. A village is small and has few people. And a town is somewhere in the middle. A city might have over 100,000 people. A town might have around 20,000-50,000 people. And a village usually has fewer than 1,000 people.

But there is a clearer difference between them. In the United States, a city is an **incorporated community**. This means it has a government. There is a **mayor**, a city **council**, and other officials. Towns and villages do not have any governmental power. In the United States, a city also usually has a charter. A charter is a special **legal** document. It says that the community is a city, not a town. A village is usually a small collection of farming families. There may be some small stores and gas stations. But it doesn't have department stores or movie theaters, which a city or a town may have.

So, where do you live? A city, a town, or a village? Words 203

Vocabulary in Context   Write the words in bold next to their correct definitions.

1. _____ related with the law
2. _____ having a legal status
3. _____ the elected head of a city
4. _____ a group of people living in the same place
5. _____ a group of elected people who manage a city

Reading Comprehension

1 **What is this passage mainly about?**

   a. how a town becomes a city

   b. why people want to live in cities

   c. some famous cities around the world

   d. differences between types of communities

2 **What kind of community has fewer than 1,000 people?**

_____

3 **What is the purpose of a charter according to the passage?**

   a. to explain the rules of the city

   b. to say that the community is a city

   c. to choose the mayor of a city

   d. to open a large business, like a mall

4 **Which is NOT true according to the passage?**

   a. A city is an incorporated community.

   b. Towns do not have one million people.

   c. In the U.S., a village has a charter.

   d. A village does not have big department stores.

5 **According to the passage, what can you guess about towns?**

   a. They can be as big as cities.

   b. They are far away from villages.

   c. They can be bigger than cities.

   d. They have more stores than villages do.

Reading Skill *Comparing and contrasting is a way to explain how two or more things are similar and different.*

Fill in the chart with the words in the box.

City	Town	Village
• more than ❶_____ people • has a government and ❷_____ • has department stores or movie theaters	• around 20,000-50,000 people • doesn't have ❸_____ power and a charter • has department stores or movie theaters	• ❹_____ than 1,000 people • a group of ❺_____ families • doesn't have department stores or movie theaters

fewer   a charter   100,000   farming   governmental

Summary

Use the words in the box to complete the summary.

legal	council	government	incorporated	movie theaters

There are some important differences between cities, towns, and villages. A city is a community that has been ❶_____. This means it has a ❷_____. There is a mayor and a city ❸_____. A city also has a charter, which gives it certain ❹_____ rights under the law. Towns are smaller than cities, and they have no governmental power. Villages are smaller than towns, and they don't have department stores or ❺_____, which cities or towns may have.

Vocabulary Expansion

A The suffix "-al" means "relating to." It turns nouns into adjectives. Add "-al" to the words in the box and match each word to a definition in the chart.

accident	region	government

Words	Definition
_____	relating to a region
_____	connected with government
_____	happening in a way that is not planned

B Fill in the blanks using the words in bold from the passage. Change the forms if necessary.

1. My hometown was _____ as a city in 1950.
2. The _____ agreed to build a new school.
3. Our city's _____ was elected last year and he's a good leader.
4. Our _____ is quite small, but it has some nice parks and shops.
5. I would like to go into the _____ field. I will become a lawyer.

Theme | *History*
Reading Skill | *Categorizing*

Unit 10

Starbucks of the 18th Century

Before You Read

A How do you communicate with your friends? Answer the questions.

1. Do you use Internet sites like Facebook and Twitter?
2. How often do you call your friends on the phone?
3. Do you like to meet your friends in coffee shops or restaurants?

B Look at the vocabulary and check the ones you know.

☐ relax   ☐ public   ☐ politics
☐ sneak   ☐ composer ☐ dress up

Starbucks of the 18th Century

▶ As you read, focus on the importance of coffeehouses to 18th-century life.

These days, we use social media to share information and ideas. We have Twitter, Facebook, instant messaging, and other sites. There were none of those things in the 18th century. So where did people go to talk back then?

In those days, educated men went to coffeehouses to talk. In Europe, coffeehouses were like the Facebook of the 18th century. Every city had many coffeehouses. Men often went there to talk about the news of the day. Coffeehouses were filled with exciting talks about life and **politics**. Many great composers, artists, and writers of the time also enjoyed spending their days in coffeehouses. The composer Johann Sebastian Bach even wrote a song about the joys of the coffeehouse.

Women usually had to stay at home. They were not allowed to go to coffeehouses with the men. But some women did not let that stop them. They often **dressed up** in men's clothes. Then they **sneaked** into the coffeehouse for a cup of coffee or two!

Coffeehouses do not have that **public** importance anymore. Nowadays, they are just places to **relax** with a cup of coffee. So it can be difficult for us to imagine how exciting they used to be. **Words 200**

Vocabulary in Context

Write the words and phrases in bold next to their correct definitions.

1. _____ to move quietly
2. _____ activities of government
3. _____ to rest and enjoy yourself
4. _____ able to be used by anyone; not private
5. _____ to wear special clothes to pretend to be somebody else

Reading Comprehension

1 What is the main idea of this passage?

a. 18th-century politics were hard to understand.
b. Coffee was a very popular drink in the 18th century.
c. 18th-century coffeehouses were like the social media of today.
d. In the 18th century, only men had the freedom to enjoy meeting in public.

2 What did men talk about in coffeehouses in the 18th century?

_____

3 What did Bach do to show his love for coffeehouses?

a. He wrote a song about them.
b. He performed at them.
c. He wrote an article about them.
d. He opened his own coffeehouse.

4 Which is NOT true about 18th-century coffeehouses?

a. People talked about politics in coffeehouses.
b. There were many coffeehouses in every city.
c. Women were allowed to go to coffeehouses.
d. Artists and writers often went to coffeehouses.

5 According to the passage, what can you guess about the 18th century?

a. Women went out quite often.
b. There were not many places to talk.
c. People often played music at coffeehouses.
d. Women did not understand politics well.

Reading Skill *Categorizing information means to arrange information or items into different groups.*

Fill in the chart with the words in the box.

The 18th Century	Nowadays
• Every European city had coffeehouses where ❶_____ gathered to talk. • There were exciting conversations about ❷_____ and the news. • Women were not ❸_____, but some sneaked in dressed as men.	• People go to coffeehouses mainly to drink coffee and ❹_____. • ❺_____ has replaced coffeehouses.

politics   relax   social media   educated men   allowed

Unit 10   47

Summary

Use the words and phrases in the box to complete the summary.

politics   women   public   composers   dressed up

Coffeehouses of the 18th century were exciting ❶_____ places. ❷_____, artists, and other educated men went there. They could talk about ❸_____ and other news. ❹_____ were not allowed to go. However, some women ❺_____ in men's clothes and went into coffeehouses on their own. For people in the 18th century, coffeehouses were like the social media of the time.

Vocabulary Expansion

A   Match the words with their similar and opposite meanings from the box.

worry   pleasure   social   sadness   private   take it easy

Words	Similar Meaning	Opposite Meaning
relax	_____	_____
public	_____	_____
joy	_____	_____

B   Fill in the blanks using the words and phrases in bold from the passage. Change the forms if necessary.

1. They didn't know that their dog _____ out of the house.
2. There are not many _____ phones on the street nowadays.
3. After you finish all your homework, you can _____ and watch TV.
4. I'm not interested in _____. I don't understand how governments work.
5. I don't want to eat at home tonight. Let's _____ and go out to a nice restaurant.

Theme | *Environment*
Reading Skill | *Main Idea & Details*

Unit 11

Why Trees Matter

Before You Read

A How much do you know about trees? Check *T* or *F*.

1. Trees can make the air cooler.   T / F
2. Many types of trees die if bugs live in them.   T / F
3. Trees can help people save money.   T / F

B Look at the vocabulary and check the ones you know.

☐ moist ☐ shade ☐ pollution
☐ benefit ☐ ecologist ☐ ecosystem

Why Trees Matter

▶ *As you read, pay attention to the different benefits trees provide.*

Host Welcome to *Environmental Matters*. Today, we are going to talk about the importance of trees for our world. **Ecologist** Dr. Henry Rand is going to explain why. Doctor, what would you say the greatest **benefit** of trees is?

Dr. Henry Well, trees are essential for the health of the environment. First, they reduce air **pollution**. They absorb carbon dioxide and harmful gasses, and release oxygen. Trees also keep the air **moist** and cool. My research has found that trees reduce the temperature in cities by up to 7 degrees Celsius.

Host I didn't realize trees affect the environment so much.

Dr. Henry They sure do. But that's not all. Mature trees are home to complex ecosystems. Communities of birds, insects, and fungi all call trees their home. In fact, up to 500 different species can live in a single tree!

Host That's amazing, but what about homeowners? Do trees affect them?

Dr. Henry Absolutely. For one, the *USDA found that the **shade** from trees keep homes cooler. This can reduce air conditioner usage by as much as 30 percent. Also, having beautiful trees increases the value of a home between 5 and 18 percent.

Host Wow! Trees are really important in so many ways.   **Words 195**

*USDA: United States Department of Agriculture

Vocabulary in Context   *Write the words in bold next to their correct definitions.*

1. _____ slightly wet
2. _____ a good or helpful result
3. _____ the action of making the land, water, and air dirty
4. _____ an area of darkness made when something blocks the sun
5. _____ a scientist who studies living things and the environment

Reading Comprehension

1 What is the main idea of this passage?

   a. People can save money by planting trees.
   b. Trees give many different types of advantages.
   c. Planting trees is the best way to remove pollution.
   d. Trees have many problems that people do not know about.

2 How do trees benefit the environment according to the passage?

   a. They create more carbon dioxide.
   b. They release oxygen and keep the air cool.
   c. They reduce the temperature by up to 4 degrees Celsius.
   d. They absorb air that is essential for environmental health.

3 What types of living creatures live in trees?

   _____

4 Which is NOT mentioned in the passage?

   a. what types of gasses trees absorb
   b. the number of species that live in a tree
   c. how much trees increase the value of a home
   d. types of birds and insects that live in trees

5 According to the passage, you can guess that _____.

   a. almost all types of insects live in trees
   b. people prefer air conditioners over tree shade
   c. people like to buy houses with beautiful trees
   d. carbon dioxide is the most dangerous type of pollution

Reading Skill *The main idea is usually at the beginning of a text and makes a general statement. The supporting details are specific ideas that support the main idea.*

Fill in the chart with the words in the box.

Main Idea	Trees provide a lot of ❶_____.
Details	• Trees benefit the ❷_____ by reducing air pollution. • Trees host complex ❸_____. • Trees provide advantages for ❹_____.

   ecosystems   environment   homeowners   benefits

Summary

Use the words and phrases in the box to complete the summary.

increase	air pollution	ecosystems	shade	benefits

Trees have many ❶_____ for the environment, animals, and humans. First, trees benefit the environment by removing ❷_____. This helps to make the air cool and wet. Also, trees host complex ❸_____. Birds, insects, and fungi can all live in a single tree. Finally, homeowners benefit from trees. The ❹_____ from trees keeps houses cool, lowering air conditioning bills. They also ❺_____ the value of a home.

Vocabulary Expansion

A The suffix "-ist" is used to show a person who does a specific activity. Add "-ist" to the words in the box. If the word ends in "-y," drop the "y" before adding "-ist." Then match each word to a definition in the chart.

ecology	novel	psychology

Words	Definition
_____	a person who writes books
_____	a scientist who studies the environment
_____	a scientist who studies the mind

B Fill in the blanks using the words in bold from the passage. Change the forms if necessary.

1. I like _____ cookies, but these are really dry.

2. It's too hot in the sun. Let's stand in the _____.

3. There are many _____ of eating fruits and nuts.

4. One way to reduce _____ is to use public transportation.

5. The government hired many _____ to study the park's forests.

Theme | *Social Issues*
Reading Skill | *Sequencing*

Unit 12

Penny Harvest

Before You Read

A What do you know about the Penny Harvest? Check *T* or *F*.

1. It is a program for teaching children how to save money.   T / F
2. The Penny Harvest is usually done by local banks.   T / F
3. Children collect pennies from their neighbors.   T / F

B Look at the vocabulary and check the ones you know.

☐ stray ☐ raise ☐ harvest

☐ phase ☐ so far ☐ immigrant

Penny Harvest

▶ *As you read, focus on how the Penny Harvest works.*

Every year, students of New York have a "Penny **Harvest**." A Penny Harvest is a program for teaching students how to help out in their communities.

There are three **phases** to the Penny Harvest. The first part takes place in October. Students go to their neighbors' houses with their parents and collect pennies. People often have a lot of pennies around the house. Then the students bring these pennies back to a group of student leaders.

In the second part of the project, the student leaders decide what they want to do with the money. There are also contests and activities for them. These activities help the students learn more about their communities. They learn about problems like homeless people or **stray** animals.

In the third part of the project, the students become more involved in the community and try to help solve its problems. Students have done several things so far. They have taught English to **immigrants** and planted gardens in the community.

Students of all ages enjoy the Penny Harvest. Since 1991, the Penny Harvest has **raised** over $10.5 million! Words 182

Vocabulary in Context
Write the words in bold next to their correct definitions.

1. _____ not having a home, or lost
2. _____ a stage or part of a process
3. _____ to bring or collect money together
4. _____ a person who comes to another country to live
5. _____ a time when crops are gathered from the fields

Reading Comprehension

1 What is this passage mainly about?

   a. a system of education
   b. a type of program to help immigrants
   c. a way for communities to raise money
   d. a way for students to help their communities

2 How are the pennies collected?

   _____

3 Who decides what to do with the pennies?

   a. parents   b. teachers
   c. neighbors   d. student leaders

4 Which is the third phase of the Penny Harvest?

   a. collecting pennies from their neighbors
   b. trying to solve the communities' problems
   c. deciding what to do with the collected pennies
   d. learning about some problems of their communities

5 According to the passage, what can you guess about the Penny Harvest?

   a. It costs a lot of money.
   b. It takes place in spring.
   c. It lasts for several months.
   d. It mainly helps local business.

Reading Skill   *Sequencing is putting events in order from first to last. When we sequence, we can easily understand which events happen first, second, and so on.*

Fill in the chart and number the events in order.

Three Phases to the Penny Harvest
Student leaders ❶_____ what to do with the money.
Students collect ❷_____ from their ❸_____.
The students try to help their ❹_____ solve their problems.

pennies   neighbors   decide   communities

Summary

Use the words and phrases in the box to complete the summary.

communities   phases   collect   takes place   immigrants

The Penny Harvest ❶_____ every year at schools in New York. There are three ❷_____ to the Penny Harvest. First, students ❸_____ pennies from their neighbors. Second, student leaders decide what to do with the money. Third, the students help solve problems in their ❹_____. The Penny Harvest students have taught English to ❺_____ and planted gardens.

Vocabulary Expansion

A Match the words with their similar meanings from the box.

happen   collect   homeless

Words	Similar Meaning
raise	_____
stray	_____
take place	_____

B Fill in the blanks using the words in bold from the passage. Change the forms if necessary.

1. We _____ money to help homeless families.
2. The first _____ of the project will be about research.
3. Every year, many _____ leave their countries to live in the U.S.
4. The streets are full of _____ cats and dogs. I feel so sad for them.
5. The farm _____ happens in October. That's when we collect all the crops for the year.

Theme | *Daily Life*
Reading Skill | *Cause & Effect*

Unit 13

Tips for Saving Time

Before You Read

A   Do you ever waste time? Take this quiz to find out.

1. Do you wait until later to do hard tasks?
2. Do you spend too much time doing one activity?
3. Do you ever spend time using the Internet instead of working?

B   Look at the vocabulary and check the ones you know.

☐ task   ☐ fantastic   ☐ distraction

☐ relief   ☐ efficiently   ☐ keep track of

Tips for Saving Time

▶ *As you read, focus on the different ways that people can use their time better.*

Do you ever wish you had more time to do your work? It is impossible to add more hours to the day. However, it is possible to use your time more **efficiently**. Just follow these time saving tips to get more work done.

1. Make a Schedule

Write down the activities you want to do each day. Next, write the times you want to spend doing each activity. For instance, write "Study English, 6:00-8:00." A schedule helps you **keep track of** your time. This means you won't spend too much time doing any one activity.

2. Do Your Most Difficult Activities First

Many people want to do their hardest **tasks** late in the day. This is a mistake. Most people are too tired to do these difficult jobs late in the day. Instead, do the most challenging tasks first. You'll have more energy to do them well. Plus, you'll feel **relief** after finishing them.

3. Turn Off the Internet

The Internet is a fantastic learning tool. It is also a big **distraction**. When you have to concentrate on a task, turn off the Internet. That way, you won't waste time online reading comics, watching videos, or using social media. **Words 199**

Vocabulary in Context
Write the words and phrases in bold next to their correct definitions.

1. _____ a job for someone to do
2. _____ to watch or follow the process of
3. _____ done without wasting time or energy
4. _____ a pleasant feeling after something stressful stops
5. _____ something that makes it difficult to think or pay attention

Reading Comprehension

1 **What is this passage mainly about?**

a. ways to do tasks more efficiently

b. methods to help people feel relief

c. why using the Internet helps learning

d. how people should keep track of the time

2 **Why is it important to make a schedule?**

_____

3 **It is easier to do difficult activities earlier in the day because** _____.

a. we have more time

b. we do not have to worry

c. we feel more energetic

d. we can feel more stress

4 **Which is NOT mentioned as a way people waste time online?**

a. using social media

b. listening to music

c. watching videos

d. reading online comics

5 **According to the passage, you can guess that** _____.

a. many people use their time efficiently

b. hard jobs are easier to do later in the day

c. the first step in saving time is making a schedule

d. people use the Internet only to distract themselves

Reading Skill   *Cause and effect is when one event causes something to happen. The cause explains why something happens, and the effect is what happens as a result.*

Fill in the chart with the words in the box.

Cause	Effect
Make a ❶_____ of each day's events.	You can keep track of the time you ❷_____ doing each activity.
Do the ❸_____ activities first in the day.	You will have more ❹_____ to do them.
Turn off the Internet when you have to concentrate on a task.	You will not ❺_____ time doing other, less important activities.

waste   hardest   schedule   spend   energy

Unit 13   59

Summary

Use the words and phrases in the box to complete the summary.

certain time   relaxed   turn off   efficiently   difficult

Many people have trouble using their time ❶_____. One way to save time is to make a schedule of your activities. This will help you to finish your jobs within a ❷_____. Another way to save time is to do the most ❸_____ activities early. If you do your hardest tasks first, you will have more energy and feel ❹_____ after doing them. Finally, make sure you ❺_____ the Internet. This means you will not waste time looking at comics or using social media.

Vocabulary Expansion

A You can add "-ly" to adjectives and make them adverbs. Change the forms and fill in the blanks.

Adjective	Adverb	Adjective	Adverb
efficient	_____	beautiful	_____
dangerous	_____	proud	_____

B Fill in the blanks using the words and phrases in bold from the passage. Change the forms if necessary.

1. Your first _____ is solving these math problems.

2. I felt a great sense of _____ after my tests were over.

3. Could you please stop talking while I study? It's a big _____.

4. You should _____ what you eat to help you lose weight.

5. To work _____, you need to do your work as quickly as possible.

Theme | *Mysteries*
Reading Skill | *Sequencing*

Unit 14

The Amber Room

▲ The Catherine Palace that has the reproduced Amber Room

Before You Read

A What do you know about World War II? Check *T* or *F*.

1. It was fought during the 1910s.   T / F
2. The Russians and Germans were enemies.   T / F
3. The Nazis controlled Germany during the time.   T / F

B Look at the vocabulary and check the ones you know.

☐ royal ☐ amber ☐ amaze
☐ precious ☐ decorate ☐ take over

The Amber Room

▶ As you read, focus on what happened to the Amber Room.

▲ A stamp showing the Amber Room

The *Amber Room was a beautiful, expensive room built in Prussia in the early 18th century. It was called "the Amber Room" because builders used a lot of amber to **decorate** it.

The room was decorated with amber panels and gold leaves on the walls. It was filled with **precious** stones and beautiful furniture. Historians believe the room was worth about $140 million in today's money. Russian **royals** used the room for different things. Some used the room as a place to think. Others brought guests there.

For over 200 years, the room **amazed** everyone. But in World War II, the Nazis **took over** Russia. Russian officials tried to move the room but they couldn't. Amber is not a strong material. It is easy to break. The Russians covered the room with wallpaper, but the Nazis found it anyway. They took the room apart and shipped it to Germany. After that, the room disappeared completely.

Most historians believe the room was destroyed in 1944. However, some people say the room still exists. This theory got special attention when a piece from the Amber Room was found in 1997 in Germany. Even so, nobody really knows what happened to it.   Words 199

*amber: an orange-yellow material to make jewelry

▲ amber

Vocabulary in Context

Write the words and phrases in bold next to their correct definitions.

1. _____ very valuable
2. _____ to surprise greatly
3. _____ to take control of something
4. _____ a member of the family of a king or queen
5. _____ to make something look better by putting other things on it

Reading Comprehension

1 **What is this passage mainly about?**

  a. how the Nazis took over Russia
  b. how the Amber Room disappeared
  c. how amber was used to decorate a room
  d. how a room can be beautifully decorated

2 **What did the royals use the Amber Room for?**

  _____

3 **What happened to the Amber Room in World War II?**

  a. The Russians built it.
  b. The Nazis took pictures of it.
  c. The Nazis took it to Germany.
  d. The Russians broke it into pieces.

4 **Which is NOT true about the Amber Room?**

  a. Russian officials failed to move it.
  b. It was built a few months before World War II.
  c. It was filled with beautiful stones and furniture.
  d. Its walls were decorated with gold and amber.

5 **What can you guess about the Amber Room?**

  a. It was lost in 1997.
  b. It is hidden in Russia.
  c. Russians were proud of it.
  d. Historians know where it is.

Reading Skill *Sequencing is putting events in order from first to last. When we sequence, we can easily understand which events happen first, second, and so on.*

Fill in the chart and number the events in order.

The Nazis ❶_____ Russia during World War II.	
The Amber Room was ❷_____ with amber and gold.	
Russian ❸_____ used the room for different things.	
The Nazis stole the room and no one knows what ❹_____ to it.	

  decorated   happened   took over   royals

Summary

Use the words in the box to complete the summary.

precious   meeting   shipped   decorated   amazed

In the 18th century, a beautiful room was built out of amber in Prussia. Russian royals used the room for thinking and ❶_____ guests. The room was ❷_____ with ❸_____ stones and gold leaves. It ❹_____ and impressed everyone who saw it. When the Nazis took over Russia during World War II, they stole the room. They ❺_____ it to Germany. Now, no one knows where it is.

Vocabulary Expansion

A **Match the words with their similar meanings from the box.**

valuable   adorn   surprise

Words	Similar Meaning
decorate	_____
precious	_____
amaze	_____

B **Fill in the blanks using the words and phrases in bold from the passage. Change the forms if necessary.**

1. My family are the most _____ people in my life.
2. I was _____ by the size of the Empire State Building.
3. In the 12th century, Genghis Khan _____ most of Asia.
4. The children _____ the Christmas tree with colorful balls and lights.
5. The most famous _____ in the world are Prince William and his wife Kate.

Theme | *Astronomy*
Reading Skill | *Categorizing*

Unit **15**

Where Did the Moon Come from?

Before You Read

A What do you know about the moon? Check *T* or *F*.

1. There are many theories about the origin of the moon.   T / F
2. The moon travels around the sun like the planets do.   T / F
3. The moon doesn't have any plants on it.   T / F

B Look at the vocabulary and check the ones you know.

☐ capture   ☐ theory   ☐ physicist

☐ crash   ☐ gravity   ☐ collision

Where Did the Moon Come from?

▶ *As you read, focus on some ideas about where the moon came from.*

Roberta — Today we're talking to **physicist** Dr. Harvey Hamelin about the origin of the moon. Can you tell us where the moon came from?

Dr. Hamelin — That's actually kind of a mystery, Roberta. There are several **theories** about the origin of the moon, but no one knows for sure. Probably the most popular theory is that another planet **crashed** into the Earth about 4.5 billion years ago, and the moon formed from the pieces of rock left behind.

Roberta — Are there any other theories about it?

Dr. Hamelin — Well, another idea is that it formed elsewhere in the solar system. Then it came close enough for Earth's **gravity** to capture it. This is how other larger planets captured their smaller moons. Another theory claims that the Earth and the moon were actually formed at the same time, from a **collision** of two other planets.

Roberta — Thank you, Dr. Hamelin. Can you tell us any other interesting facts about the moon?

Dr. Hamelin — People think the moon is a lot closer than it really is. But it's actually nearly 400,000 kilometers away. That's like 100 trips from New York to Los Angeles. That's really, really far away! **Words 191**

Vocabulary in Context   *Write the words in bold next to their correct definitions.*

1. _____ to hit something else very hard
2. _____ a scientific explanation for something
3. _____ an accident where two objects hit each other
4. _____ the force that causes things to fall towards the Earth
5. _____ a scientist who studies nature and how objects move

Reading Comprehension

1 What is the main idea of this passage?

   a. People have always been fascinated by the moon.
   b. No one really knows where the moon came from.
   c. The moon was formed by crashing into another planet.
   d. The moon is much farther away from the Earth than most people think.

2 What is the most popular theory about where the moon came from?

   a. It was created at the same time as the Earth.
   b. It was created by a giant volcano on the Earth.
   c. It was created when a planet crashed into the Earth.
   d. It was created when the Earth captured a smaller planet.

3 According to the passage, what keeps the moon close to the Earth?

   a. collisions
   b. gravity
   c. another planet
   d. the solar system

4 How far away is the moon from the Earth?

   _____

5 What can you guess from the passage?

   a. The moon is smaller than the Earth.
   b. The Earth and the moon are the same age.
   c. Scientists know where the moon came from.
   d. Dr. Hamelin believes the moon formed somewhere else in the solar system.

Reading Skill *Categorizing information means to arrange information or items into different groups.*

Fill in the chart with the words in the box.

Theory 1	Another planet crashed into the Earth. The moon was formed by large ❶_____ of rock from the crash.
Theory 2	The moon was formed in another part of space. Then, it came ❷_____ to the Earth and Earth's gravity captured it.
Theory 3	❸_____ and the moon formed at the same time when two different planets crashed into ❹_____.

the Earth   close   each other   pieces

Unit 15 67

Summary

Use the words in the box to complete the summary.

| formed | collision | physicists | gravity | theories |

Many ❶_____ are still not certain how the moon was ❷_____. They have many ❸_____ about it, though. Some think the moon was captured by Earth's ❹_____. Others think another planet crashed into the Earth, and the collision formed the moon. Another theory claims that the Earth and the moon were actually formed at the same time from a ❺_____ of two other planets. But no one is really sure.

Vocabulary Expansion

A Match the words with their similar meanings from the box.

| create | hit | catch |

Words	Similar Meaning
crash	_____
form	_____
capture	_____

B Fill in the blanks using the words in bold from the passage. Change the forms if necessary.

1. Stephen Hawking is a world-famous _____.
2. The rock _____ through the window and fell to the floor.
3. There was a car accident today, but no one was hurt in the _____.
4. Newton made his idea about _____ when he saw a falling apple.
5. Nobody knows who robbed the bank, but the police have a _____: more than one person did it.

Theme | *Technology*
Reading Skill | *Cause & Effect*

Unit 16

The Mysterious Box on Airplanes

Before You Read

A What do you know about black boxes? Check *T* or *F*.

1. They are only found on airplanes.   T / F
2. They have food in them.   T / F
3. They really are black.   T / F

B Look at the vocabulary and check the ones you know.

☐ locate   ☐ crash   ☐ spot
☐ cockpit   ☐ flight   ☐ copilot

The Mysterious Box on Airplanes

▶ *As you read, focus on the functions of black boxes in airplanes.*

Have you ever heard a news report about an airplane **crash** and the reporter said, "Officials are still searching for the black box"? Most people know that the black box is important. However, they really don't know much about what it does or how it's used in a **flight**.

First of all, the black box isn't even really black. It's actually bright orange in color. This makes it very easy to **spot** when officials are searching the ground or ocean for it. The black box is **located** in the tail of the plane. In a crash, the tail usually receives the smallest amount of damage.

The black box records everything that happens in the cockpit during a

flight. It records conversations between the pilot and **copilots**, changes in the flight, and many other important details. Thus, after a crash, we can find out what happened.

Black boxes were first put in airplanes in 1967. They help us understand how crashes can happen. That way, we can learn from our mistakes and build better and safer airplanes.

Words 176

Vocabulary in Context
Write the words in bold next to their correct definitions.

1. _____ to see; to notice
2. _____ to put in a particular place
3. _____ the airplane that is making a journey
4. _____ the person who helps the pilot fly the plane
5. _____ an accident where a plane or a car is seriously damaged

Reading Comprehension

1 **What is the main idea of this passage?**

a. Plane crashes are often a complete mystery.

b. Black boxes are a danger to every airplane passenger.

c. Black boxes help us find out what happened in a plane crash.

d. Pilots and copilots need to work together to keep passengers safe.

2 **What color is a black box?**

_____

3 **Where are black boxes located on the plane?**

a. in the tail

b. in the aisle

c. in the cockpit

d. in the bathroom

4 **Which is NOT true according to the passage?**

a. The tail of a plane receives the least damage.

b. Black boxes record conversations in the cockpit.

c. Black boxes were first put in airplanes in the 1940s.

d. The color of black boxes helps officials to easily spot them.

5 **According to the passage, what can you guess about black boxes?**

a. They are used by the copilot.

b. They receive a lot of damage.

c. They have a lot of different uses.

d. They help make air travel safer.

Reading Skill *Cause and effect is when one event causes something to happen. The cause explains why something happens, and the effect is what happens as a result.*

Fill in the chart with the words in the box.

Cause	Effect
Black boxes are orange.	They can be easily ❶_____ in a crash.
The ❷_____ of the plane receives the ❸_____ damage.	Black boxes are located in the ❷_____.
Black boxes record important ❹_____ during a flight.	They can help us find out what ❺_____.

least   tail   happened   spotted   details

Summary

Use the words in the box to complete the summary.

spot   located   crash   happened   records

In a plane ❶_____, officials usually search for a black box. This black box tells them what happened to the plane. The black box is actually orange because orange is easier to ❷_____. The black box is ❸_____ in the tail of the plane and ❹_____ everything that happens in the flight. It records conversations between the pilot and copilots. This helps officials learn how the crash ❺_____.

Vocabulary Expansion

A   Match the words and phrases with their similar meanings from the box.

collision   notice   look for

Words	Similar Meaning
spot	_____
crash	_____
search for	_____

B   Fill in the blanks using the words in bold from the passage. Change the forms if necessary.

1. Our _____ to Beijing leaves at 4 p.m.
2. Our new restaurant is _____ on the corner.
3. There was a bad car _____ on Highway 112 this morning.
4. The police _____ a black van speeding along the highway.
5. Every airplane pilot needs a _____ to help him fly the plane.

Theme | *Nature*
Reading Skill | *Sequencing*

Unit **17**

Wasps Help Protect Corn

Before You Read

A **What do you know about wasps? Check *T* or *F*.**

1. Wasps like to eat corn. T / F
2. Wasps attack other bugs. T / F
3. Many people are afraid of wasps. T / F

B **Look at the vocabulary and check the ones you know.**

☐ wasp ☐ defense ☐ entire

☐ sting ☐ fascinating ☐ protect

Unit 17 **73**

Wasps Help Protect Corn

▶ *As you read, focus on the signals that corn sends to wasps.*

Most people hate wasps. They are very dangerous and can **sting** many times. But wasps are actually very important in nature.

Wasps help to **protect** corn from being eaten. The way they do this is like something out of a science fiction movie. Corn is a very popular food for many small insects and worms. But corn has an amazing **defense** system against these hungry bugs. When a certain kind of worm is eating it, corn sends out a chemical into the air. If a different kind of worm is eating it, the corn can send out a different chemical. This chemical calls wasps that attack that kind of worm. Without these wasps, the worms would eat the **entire** crop of corn.

These chemicals are called "volatiles." The plant sends out a cloud of these chemicals, which have a special smell. The wasps are then easily able to find the correct plant. The chemicals also tell the wasp what kind of bug is eating the corn. So the wasp quickly finds the bug that it eats.

Corn needs protection against bugs, so corn and wasps developed a way to communicate with each other. It's a **fascinating** relationship.   *Words 197*

Vocabulary in Context
Write the words in bold next to their correct definitions.

1. _____ all; complete
2. _____ very interesting
3. _____ to keep from harm
4. _____ a way to stop something from attacking
5. _____ to cause pain with a sharp part that usually has poison

Reading Comprehension

1 What is the main idea of this passage?

    a. Corn actually seems to be able to think.
    b. Wasps and corn have a beneficial relationship.
    c. Wasps are causing big problems all over the world.
    d. Chemicals in corn are what make it so delicious.

2 What do the chemicals do?

    a. They help protect the corn against wasps.
    b. They kill the bugs that are eating the corn.
    c. They kill the wasps that are attacking the corn.
    d. They call the wasps to come and protect the corn.

3 How do the chemicals help wasps to find the correct plant?

_____

4 Which is NOT mentioned in the passage?

    a. where wasps lay their eggs
    b. how wasps protect corn from attackers
    c. the danger that bugs can cause corn
    d. the name of the chemicals that corn sends

5 What can you guess from the passage?

    a. Corn grows taller where many bugs are.
    b. Corn knows what kinds of bugs are eating it.
    c. The chemicals called volatiles kill bugs that eat corn.
    d. Wasps can communicate with worms and other bugs.

Reading Skill *Sequencing is putting events in order from first to last. When we sequence, we can easily understand which events happen first, second, and so on.*

Fill in the chart and number the events in order.

The corn sends out ❶_____ signals.
Wasps find the corn and ❷_____ the worms.
Worms start ❸_____ the corn.
Wasps smell the chemical ❹_____.

    signals   eating   chemical   attack

Summary

Use the words and phrases in the box to complete the summary.

| fascinating | wasps | defense | sends out | entire |

Corn and wasps have a unique relationship. When corn is being eaten by worms, it has an amazing ❶_____ system. It ❷_____ a cloud of chemicals called volatiles. ❸_____ smell the chemicals and fly to where the corn is. Then, the wasps eat the worms. That way, the worms don't eat the ❹_____ crop of the corn. It is a ❺_____ relationship.

Vocabulary Expansion

A Match the words with their similar meanings from the box.

| whole | interesting | protection |

Words	Similar Meaning
defense	_____
entire	_____
fascinating	_____

B Fill in the blanks using the words in bold from the passage. Change the forms if necessary.

1. Wasps will _____ if they are disturbed.

2. A winter coat _____ you from the cold weather.

3. Don't eat the _____ bag of cookies. Just have one or two.

4. The best _____ we have against car accidents is safe driving.

5. I saw a _____ movie about World War II last night. I learned a lot.

Theme | *Sports*
Reading Skill | *Categorizing*

Unit 18

Weird Sports

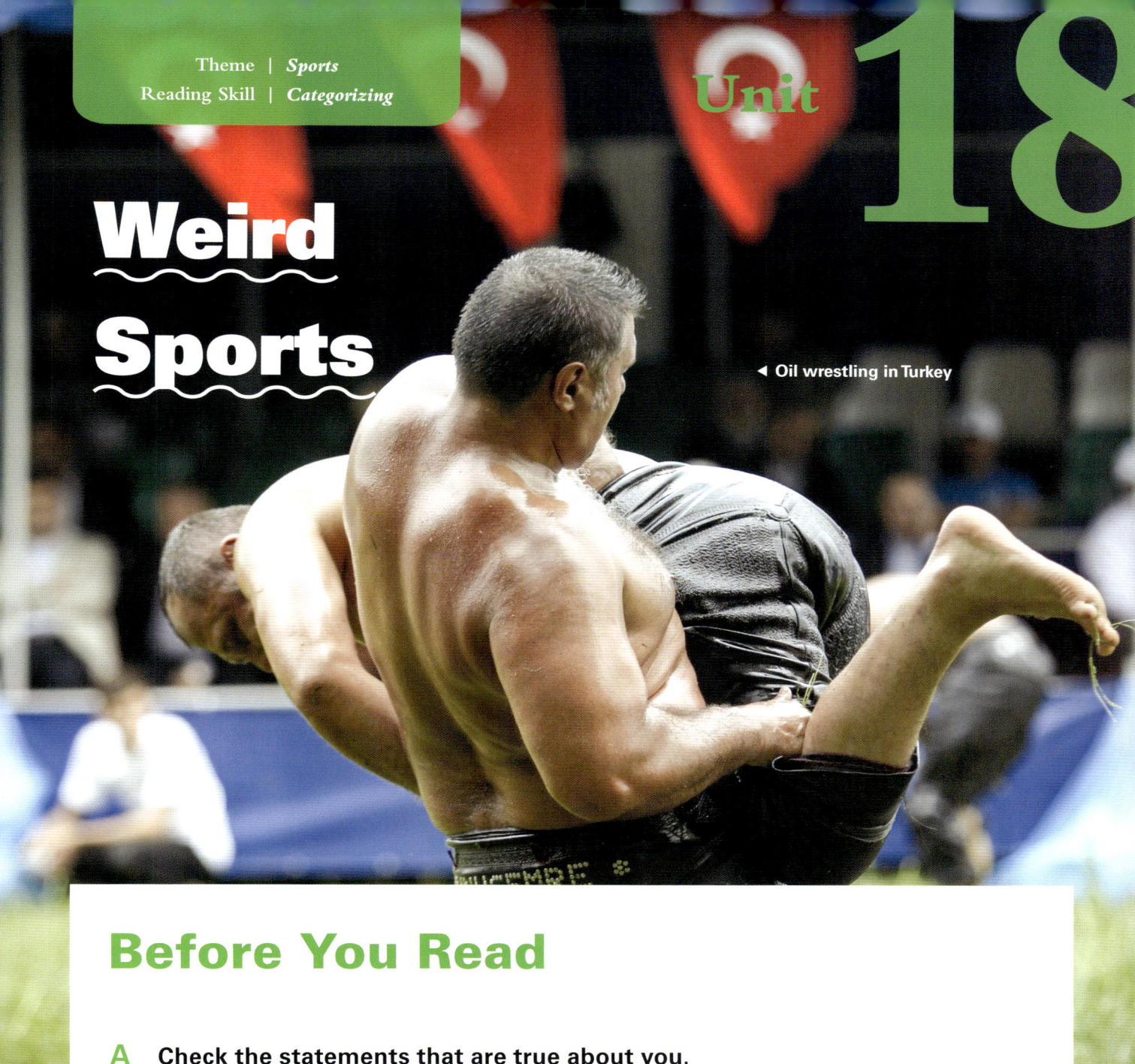

◀ Oil wrestling in Turkey

Before You Read

A Check the statements that are true about you.

☐ 1. I enjoy playing sports.
☐ 2. I am interested in trying new and different kinds of sports.
☐ 3. When I play sports, I sometimes change the rules to make them more fun.

B Look at the vocabulary and check the ones you know.

☐ obstacle   ☐ course   ☐ predictable
☐ slippery   ☐ originate   ☐ competition

Unit 18 · 77

Weird Sports

▶ *As you read, focus on how these weird sports are different from regular sports.*

For most people, sports like soccer, basketball, and baseball are exciting enough. For other people, these sports are boring and **predictable**. These people have chosen to create new, unusual sports.

If regular wrestling is not challenging enough for you, then you should try oil wrestling. Oil wrestling is a very old sport. The first competition was held in 1362 in Turkey. The rules are simple. Participants cover their bodies in olive oil to make themselves **slippery**. Then, they try to wrestle the other players to the ground. The last wrestler standing is the winner. Oil wrestling festivals take place in Northern Greece, as well as in the Netherlands and Japan.

Do you want a sport that you can play with your wife? Then wife carrying is the sport for you. Wife carrying **originated** in Finland. It became an official sport in 1992. In the competition, a man must carry a woman through a **course** as fast as possible. The course includes **obstacles** such as sand pits, fences, and a pool. The man to finish the course fastest is the winner. Wife carrying has become popular in the United States, Australia, the United Kingdom, and Hong Kong. **Words 196**

Vocabulary in Context

Write the words in bold next to their correct definitions.

1. _____ to be produced or created
2. _____ a path or track used during a race
3. _____ something that makes it difficult to continue
4. _____ able to be guessed or known ahead of time
5. _____ difficult to stand on because of water, ice, or oil

Reading Comprehension

1 What is this passage mainly about?

a. reasons that people play unusual sports
b. the types of people who enjoy playing sports
c. ways to make old sports new and more interesting
d. strange sports that not many people know about

2 Why do oil wrestlers cover their bodies in olive oil?

_____

3 Which is NOT true about oil wrestling according to the passage?

a. It was first held in Turkey.
b. It is impossible for one person to win.
c. It is more than 650 years old.
d. It takes place in the Netherlands and Japan.

4 Participants in wife carrying must _____.

a. go to Finland in order to compete
b. pass through sand pits and a pool
c. carry their wives as long as possible
d. finish the race before their wives do

5 What can you guess about most weird sports from the passage?

a. that they are official sports
b. that they were created just a few years ago
c. that only professional players can play them
d. that people in many countries can enjoy them

Reading Skill *Categorizing information means to arrange information or items into different groups.*

Fill in the chart with the words in the box.

Oil Wrestling	Wife Carrying
• It is originally from ❶_____ in 1362. • Participants cover themselves in ❷_____ and wrestle others to the ground. • The last wrestler ❸_____ is the winner.	• It started in Finland in 1992. • Participants must carry their wives through an ❹_____ course. • The winner completes the course the ❺_____.

standing   obstacle   olive oil   Turkey   fastest

Summary

Use the words in the box to complete the summary.

carry	Finland	unusual	wins	wrestle

For some people, normal sports are boring. This is why they have created ❶_____ sports. One unusual sport is oil wrestling. It started in Turkey over 650 years ago. Participants cover themselves in olive oil and try to ❷_____ the other players to the ground. The last wrestler still standing is the winner. Another weird sport is wife carrying. This sport comes from ❸_____. Men have to ❹_____ their wives through an obstacle course. The fastest man ❺_____.

Vocabulary Expansion

A Match the words with their similar meanings from the box.

barrier	expected	contest

Words	Similar Meaning
predictable	_____
competition	_____
obstacle	_____

B Fill in the blanks using the words in bold from the passage. Change the forms if necessary.

1. The race _____ is five kilometers long.
2. To succeed in life, you must overcome many _____.
3. Be careful! The sidewalk is _____ during the winter.
4. I'm tired of watching this TV show. It's become too _____.
5. This candy _____ from Germany, but it is sold everywhere now.

Theme | *Technology*
Reading Skill | *Categorizing*

Unit 19

The Future of Travel

Before You Read

A How do you think we will travel in the future? Rank these ideas from 1 (very likely) to 4 (not likely).

_____ flying cars   _____ private spaceships
_____ computer-driven cars   _____ trains that can go 1,000 kilometers an hour

B Look at the vocabulary and check the ones you know.

☐ aircraft   ☐ decade   ☐ magnetic
☐ improve   ☐ currently   ☐ passenger

The Future of Travel

▶ *As you read, focus on ideas for future travel.*

For **decades**, people believed that someday we would drive in flying cars. Nowadays that dream seems like it will never happen. But scientists and engineers are working on the problem. They want to **improve** transportation for the future. They have a lot of ideas about how to make future travel faster and safer.

One idea is to develop self-driving cars. These cars would be driven by computers. People would become **passengers** and just enjoy the trip. NASA is coming up with another idea. It is **currently** building a new type of monorail for city travel. This train, called a SkyTran, would use **magnetic** power. This power holds individual train cars to the tracks. People will be able to move around the city at 240 kilometers an hour.

And yes, flying cars may still happen. Engineers are designing a light aircraft that changes into a car. You can drive to the airport, and change your car into an airplane. Then you fly to another airport, and change back into a car. At least, that's the idea. It may be a long time before flying cars are a reality! **Words 187**

Vocabulary in Context

Write the words in bold next to their correct definitions.

1. _____ to make better
2. _____ now; at this time
3. _____ a period of ten years
4. _____ a person who rides in a vehicle
5. _____ able to attract with electric charge

Reading Comprehension

1 What is the main idea of this passage?

   a. Someday, everyone will travel on magnetic trains.
   b. Flying cars are impossible and will never be invented.
   c. Future travel will be much easier and cheaper than now.
   d. Scientists are working on many ideas for future travel.

2 What drives self-driving cars?

   _____

3 Which is NOT true about SkyTran?

   a. It moves very fast.   b. It uses magnetic power.
   c. It is being developed by NASA.   d. It is for international travel.

4 What is NOT an idea for improving transportation according to the passage?

   a. cars that can fly between airports   b. cars that drive people everywhere
   c. cars that travel on magnetic tracks   d. cars that can travel on top of water

5 According to the passage, what can you guess about future travel?

   a. All future vehicles will use magnetic power.
   b. It will only be a few years before we will all have flying cars.
   c. Scientists are always trying to find ways to improve travel.
   d. In the future, people will all be passengers in vehicles, not drivers.

Reading Skill _Categorizing information means to arrange information or items into different groups._

Fill in the chart with the words in the box.

Vehicles for Future Travel	
Self-Driving Cars	• Self-driving cars will use ❶_____. • People will be ❷_____, not drivers.
SkyTran	• It will go 240 kilometers an hour. • It uses ❸_____ and people will ride in ❹_____ cars.
Flying Cars	• Scientists are working on a car that turns into an ❺_____. • People will be able to fly in their own cars.

passengers   airplane   magnetic power   individual   computers

Summary

Use the words and phrases in the box to complete the summary.

hold	computers	change	magnetic power	travel

Scientists and engineers are constantly working on new ways of improving ❶_____. They've been working on flying cars for decades now, and they have many other ideas too. Maybe someday ❷_____ will drive our cars, and we will become passengers. Scientists are also currently working on a train that runs on ❸_____. This power will ❹_____ the train cars to the tracks. Finally, we may all have cars that ❺_____ into aircraft.

Vocabulary Expansion

A Match the words and phrases with their similar meanings from the box.

at present	produce	develop

Words	Similar Meaning
come up with	_____
improve	_____
currently	_____

B Fill in the blanks using the words in bold from the passage. Change the forms if necessary.

1. It will be sunny later, but _____ it's raining.
2. This new plane can carry over 300 _____.
3. You can _____ your muscles by working out.
4. The clock has a _____ back so it can stick to the fridge.
5. This year is 2016. A _____ ago, in 2006, I was living in France.

Theme | *People*
Reading Skill | *Sequencing*

Unit 20

The Power of a Dream

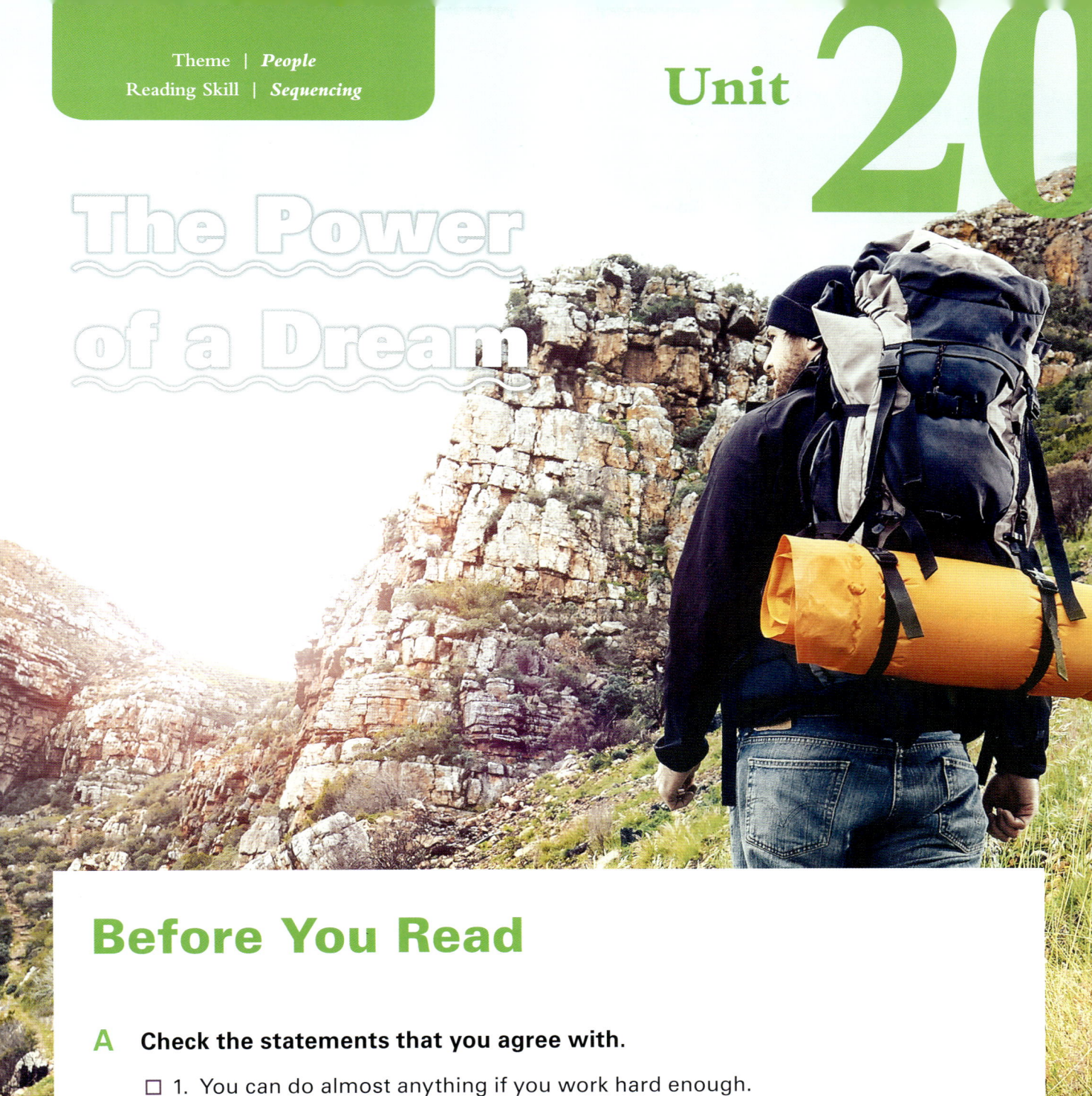

Before You Read

A Check the statements that you agree with.

☐ 1. You can do almost anything if you work hard enough.
☐ 2. People should always try to follow their dreams.
☐ 3. The greatest challenges have the greatest rewards.

B Look at the vocabulary and check the ones you know.

☐ paddle   ☐ achieve   ☐ exotic
☐ encourage ☐ journey   ☐ arrest

The Power of a Dream

▶ *As you read, pay attention to the different adventures Jason had on his trip.*

Jason Lewis had a dream to travel around the world using only his muscles. He started his **journey** in 1994 when he was 26. He hiked, rode a bicycle, rollerbladed, and paddled a boat with both his arms and feet. Thirteen years later, his dream came true.

Jason was born in England in 1967. He became interested in traveling in 1985. In that year, he visited Kenya, a country in Africa. His trip made him want to explore other **exotic** lands.

During his round-the-world trip, Jason had many challenging adventures. He was hit by a car in Colorado, and both his legs were broken. It took nine months for him to heal and get back on the road again. In Australia, he had to paddle fast to escape a 5-meter-long crocodile that attacked his small boat! In Egypt, he was **arrested** because the Egyptian police thought he was a spy.

During his trip, Jason visited many schools. He **encouraged** students to pursue their dreams. He always said, "Even if it is very difficult or takes a long time, try to **achieve** your dream. It is worth it." Words 187

Vocabulary in Context

Write the words in bold next to their correct definitions.

1. _____ a long trip
2. _____ to reach a goal by working hard
3. _____ very different, strange, or unusual
4. _____ to make someone more likely to do something
5. _____ to take a person away and keep the person at a police station

Reading Comprehension

1 What is the main idea of this passage?

   a. Car accidents are very common during trips.
   b. Do not try to achieve that are too long or difficult.
   c. Even if your dream seems difficult, it is worth doing.
   d. Traveling around the world is an exciting experience.

2 When did Jason become interested in exploring exotic lands?

   _____

3 What is the third paragraph mainly about?

   a. why Jason's trip was so much fun
   b. the dangers of traveling to Australia
   c. how to heal after a car accident
   d. the difficult times during Jason's trip

4 Which is true according to the passage?

   a. Jason was hit by a car in Egypt.
   b. The police in Australia thought Jason was a spy.
   c. Jason started his journey when he was a teenager.
   d. Jason told some students to pursue their dreams.

5 According to the passage, you can guess that _____.

   a. you should be careful when going to Egypt
   b. Jason did not have a time limit for his journey
   c. it is not a good idea to travel around the world
   d. Jason spent a lot of money on planes and trains

Reading Skill *Sequencing is putting events in order from first to last. When we sequence, we can easily understand which events happen first, second, and so on.*

Fill in the chart and number the events in order.

He visited ❶_____ and wanted to travel to other places.
When he was 26, he ❷_____ his journey around the world.
Jason was born in 1967 in ❸_____.
He had many ❹_____ during his journey and his ❺_____ came true in 2007.

   dream   began   Kenya   adventures   England

Unit 20 87

Summary

Use the words in the box to complete the summary.

dreams   arrested   achieved   broken   complete

Jason Lewis is a man who successfully ❶_____ his dream. He dreamed of traveling around the world by his own muscle power. The trip took him 13 years to ❷_____. He had many adventures, including being chased by a crocodile and being ❸_____ in Egypt. In Colorado, his legs were ❹_____ in a car accident, but he did not give up. He continued his trip after he healed. During his trip, he visited schools and taught students to follow their ❺_____.

Vocabulary Expansion

A Match the words with their similar meanings from the box.

accomplish   inspire   trip

Words	Similar Meaning
encourage	_____
journey	_____
achieve	_____

B Fill in the blanks using the words in bold from the passage. Change the forms if necessary.

1. We are very tired after our long _____.
2. My parents always _____ me to try new things.
3. The police _____ the criminal after a long chase.
4. Mia dreams of traveling to _____ places such as Tibet.
5. It took me many years to _____ my dream of being a singer.

Developing Background Knowledge and Reading Strategies

Reading

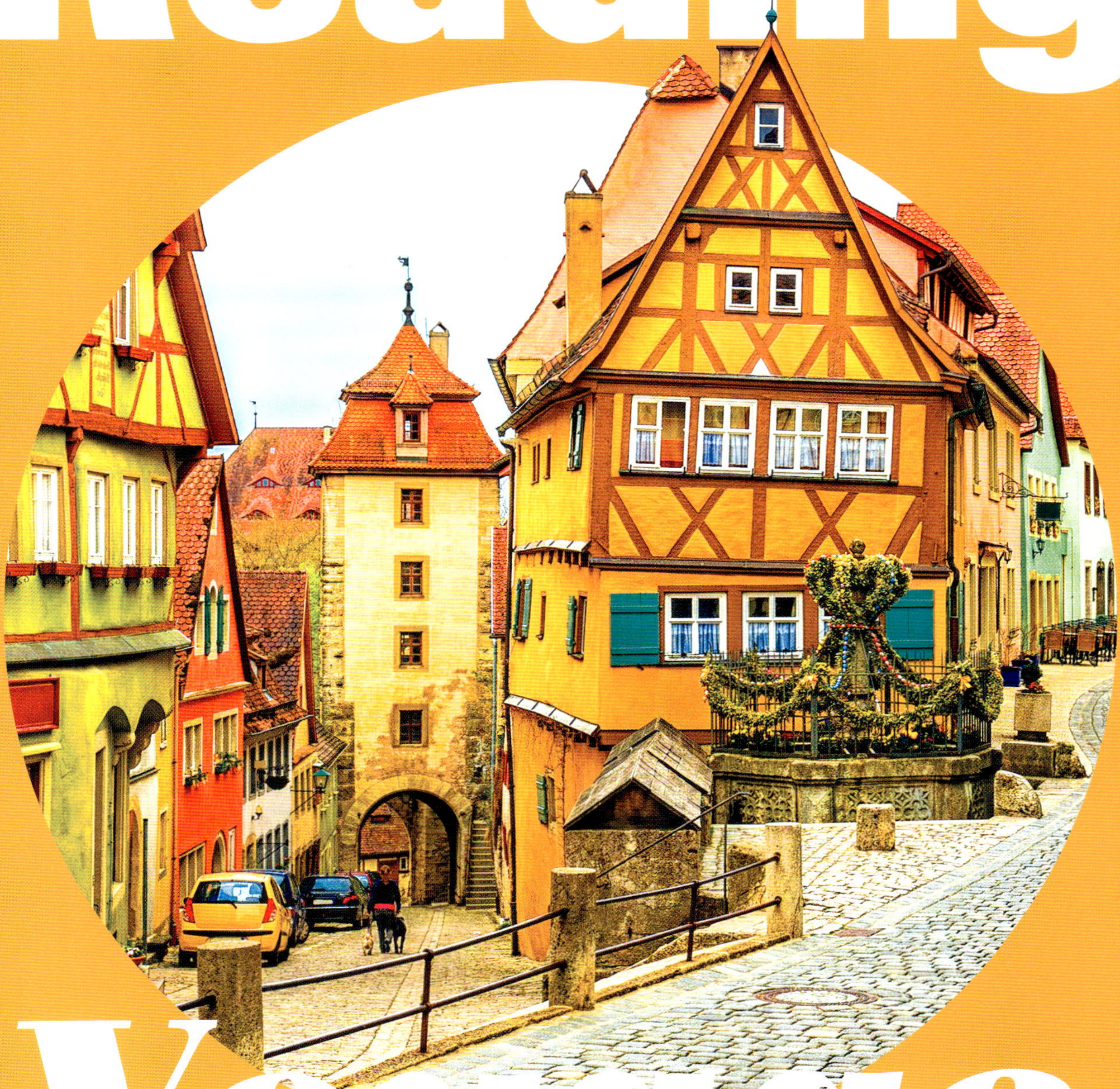

BASIC

Voyage

1

WORKBOOK

DARAKWON

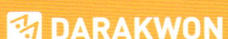

Reading Voyage

BASIC

1

WORKBOOK

Unit 1 — A Delicious British Food

Vocabulary Practice

A Write each word next to its correct definition. Then write its meaning in your language.

simmer	ingredient	fancy	mash
ground	shepherd	cuisine	brown

1. to cook on low heat _____ _____
2. to make brown by cooking _____ _____
3. to crush food into a soft mass _____ _____
4. high in quality; not plain or ordinary _____ _____
5. cut or crushed into very small pieces _____ _____
6. food that is cooked in a particular way _____ _____
7. a person whose job is to take care of sheep _____ _____
8. one of the things that is used to make a dish _____ _____

B Write the correct words to complete the sentences.

shepherd	remaining	consumed	high-quality

1. He _____ ten chocolate bars for lunch.
2. Jane always wears _____ shoes and clothes.
3. Add the _____ ingredients: sugar, salt, and eggs.
4. The _____ had to sleep near his sheep to take care of them.

Writing Practice

A Unscramble the words to complete the sentences.

1. (is / for / famous / meat pies / its)
   ➤ Britain _____.

2. (the / famous / of / most / them all)
   ➤ Cottage pie is _____.

3. (anyone / can / easy / make / meal / that)
   ➤ It's a very _____.

4. (some / until / are / potatoes / they / soft)
   ➤ Boil _____.

5. (a part / British cuisine / of / for / been / hundreds of years)
   ➤ Cottage pie has _____.

B Translate the sentences into your language, focusing on the meanings of the underlined parts.

1. Cottage pie <u>was</u> never <u>meant to</u> be a fancy meal.
   ➤ _____

2. Add the beef back to the pan and <u>pour in</u> beef stock.
   ➤ _____

3. It was just <u>a way</u> that families could <u>use up</u> their leftover meat and potatoes.
   ➤ _____

Unit 1 3

Unit 2 Repairing a Signal Tower

Vocabulary Practice

A Write each word next to its correct definition. Then write its meaning in your language.

| thin | train | rare | technician |
| pole | harness | repair | uncomfortable |

1. to fix _____ _____
2. not thick _____ _____
3. not common or usual _____ _____
4. feeling embarrassed or uneasy _____ _____
5. a long, thin piece of wood or metal _____ _____
6. to teach someone how to do something _____ _____
7. pieces of material put around the shoulders to keep a person from falling _____ _____
8. a person who is trained to fix machines or computers _____ _____

B Write the correct words to complete the sentences.

| mount | fixed | almost | thin |

1. Watch out! You're on _____ ice.
2. It's six thirty. It's _____ time to go home.
3. How do I get my car _____ after an accident?
4. Mark began to _____ the stairs with his daughter.

Writing Practice

A Unscramble the words to complete the sentences.

1. (a / climb / to / long / the top)
   ➤ It's _____.

2. (climb / a safety belt / use / to)
   ➤ They _____.

3. (need / these towers / repaired / be / to)
   ➤ Sometimes _____.

4. (scariest / top part / of / is / the / all)
   ➤ The very _____.

5. (may / a / a signal tower / dangerous / look like / job)
   ➤ Repairing _____.

B Translate the sentences into your language, focusing on the meanings of the underlined parts.

1. Some of them are <u>taller than</u> the Empire State Building.
   ➤ _____

2. <u>If a storm comes</u>, there is no quick way down, <u>except to fall</u>!
   ➤ _____

3. <u>Climbing a 540-meter tower</u> is an uncomfortable way <u>to spend</u> your working day.
   ➤ _____

Unit 3 What Does It Mean?

Vocabulary Practice

A Write each word next to its correct definition. Then write its meaning in your language.

| common | slang | type | confuse |
| opinion | humble | delete | substitute |

1. modest _____ _____

2. often used _____ _____

3. casual or playful words _____ _____

4. to write with a computer keyboard _____ _____

5. what someone thinks about something _____ _____

6. to remove a word or picture from a document _____ _____

7. to use someone or something in place of another _____ _____

8. to make someone unable to understand something _____ _____

B Write the correct words to complete the sentences.

| modest | remove | typical | arrogant |

1. Please _____ the dirty dishes from the table.

2. Terry is so _____ and doesn't like too much attention.

3. I don't want to work with him because he is _____ and rude.

4. It was just a _____ Sunday morning. Nothing special happened.

6

Writing Practice

A Unscramble the words to complete the sentences.

1. (I / it / to / type / use / faster)

   ➤ _____.

2. (means / can / guess / what / you / it)

   ➤ _____?

3. (these / fun / use / with friends / to)

   ➤ It's _____.

4. (confuse / sorry / Internet slang / with / you / to)

   ➤ I'm _____.

5. (types / two / of / are / main / Internet slang)

   ➤ There _____.

B Translate the sentences into your language, focusing on the meanings of the underlined parts.

1. You <u>must have seen</u> them before.

   ➤ _____

2. There are <u>hundreds of</u> symbols <u>called</u> emoticons.

   ➤ _____

3. People substitute numbers or letters <u>that sound like</u> words.

   ➤ _____

Unit 4 What Is Black Friday?

Vocabulary Practice

A Write each word or phrase next to its correct definition. Then write its meaning in your language.

term	rush	employer	attract
offer	traffic	take place	day off

1. to happen _____ _____
2. to provide _____ _____
3. to move or go quickly _____ _____
4. to cause to come to a place _____ _____
5. a day when you do not have to work _____ _____
6. a word or phrase to describe something _____ _____
7. a person who pays other people to work for him or her _____ _____
8. all the vehicles that are on a road at a certain time _____ _____

B Write the correct words to complete the sentences.

provides	phrase	traffic	hurried

1. Firefighters _____ to control the fire.
2. This _____ is used a lot in English culture.
3. The store _____ a quiet space for reading.
4. Take the subway to avoid _____ on Friday.

8

Writing Practice

A Unscramble the words to complete the sentences.

1. (big sales / started / on / offering / that day)
   ➤ Malls and stores _____.

2. (shopping / makes / to / it / go / a good day)
   ➤ This _____.

3. (sales / started / to / customers / having / attract)
   ➤ Stores _____.

4. (it / called / heavy traffic / "Black Friday" / because of)
   ➤ Police _____.

5. (on the day / takes place / Thanksgiving / after / in the U.S.)
   ➤ Black Friday _____

B Translate the sentences into your language, focusing on the meanings of the underlined parts.

1. Black Friday is <u>the biggest</u> shopping day in the United States.
   ➤ _____

2. People rush <u>to get</u> toys and other products <u>at the cheapest prices</u>.
   ➤ _____

3. People <u>started calling</u> the day after Thanksgiving "Black Friday" <u>in the 1950s</u>.
   ➤ _____

I Cannot Eat Peanut Butter!

Vocabulary Practice

A Write each word next to its correct definition. Then write its meaning in your language.

| rash | fool | occur | react |
| allow | pain | cure | nauseous |

1. to happen _____ _____

2. to play a trick _____ _____

3. a red spot on the skin _____ _____

4. something that gets rid of an illness _____ _____

5. to become ill after eating a certain food _____ _____

6. to let someone or something do something _____ _____

7. the feeling that you have in your body when you are sick _____ _____

8. feeling like you want to throw up; having an upset stomach _____ _____

B Write the correct words to complete the sentences.

| cheats | allowed | treatment | happened |

1. My mom _____ me to go to the party.

2. He received medical _____ for his injuries.

3. We didn't know what _____ to our neighbors.

4. I don't like playing card games with Jack because he _____.

Writing Practice

A Unscramble the words to complete the sentences.

1. (allowed / milk / is / to / not / drink)
   ➤ She _____.

2. (very / it / reacts / strongly / to)
   ➤ Your body _____.

3. (there / allergies / for / real / is / cure / no)
   ➤ _____.

4. (when / occur / is / immune system / fooled / your body's)
   ➤ Food allergies _____.

5. (in / children / food allergies / has / serious / every one hundred)
   ➤ About one _____.

B Translate the sentences into your language, focusing on the meanings of the underlined parts.

1. It is important <u>to get tested</u> for allergies when you are young.
   ➤ _____

2. Your immune system is <u>what</u> helps <u>protect you from diseases</u>.
   ➤ _____

3. Doctors can find out <u>what</u> you are allergic to <u>before</u> it has a chance <u>to make</u> you sick.
   ➤ _____

Unit 6 The Story of Narcissus

Vocabulary Practice

A Write each word or phrase next to its correct definition. Then write its meaning in your language.

spring	reject	edge	reflection
legend	delight	skinny	stumble across

1. to refuse _____ _____
2. very thin _____ _____
3. an old story; a myth _____ _____
4. to discover by accident _____ _____
5. a feeling of great happiness _____ _____
6. an image seen in a mirror or a shiny surface _____ _____
7. a place where water comes up from the ground _____ _____
8. the part where an object or area begins or ends _____ _____

B Write the correct words to complete the sentences.

education	reflection	skinny	suggestion

1. Do you agree with my _____?
2. She saw her _____ in the window of a store.
3. He gave an important speech about _____.
4. If you do not start eating more, you will always be _____.

Writing Practice

A Unscramble the words to complete the sentences.

1. (looking / time / a lot of / in / spend / a mirror)
   ➤ I _____.

2. (seen / never / had / before / his reflection)
   ➤ He _____.

3. (I / it / on / looked / the Internet / up)
   ➤ _____.

4. (he / hunting / stumbled / was / a spring / across)
   ➤ While _____, he _____.

5. (reflection / could / his / in / see / the water)
   ➤ Narcissus _____.

B Translate the sentences into your language, focusing on the meanings of the underlined parts.

1. I don't <u>want</u> others <u>to</u> see me with messy hair or a dirty face.
   ➤ _____

2. A narcissist is someone <u>who is in love with</u> his or her own beauty.
   ➤ _____

3. The name <u>comes from</u> a Greek legend about a young boy <u>named</u> Narcissus.
   ➤ _____

Unit 7 The Hottest Place in the World

Vocabulary Practice

A Write each word or phrase next to its correct definition. Then write its meaning in your language.

harsh	toxic	form	molten
annual	planet	region	all year round

1. very poisonous　　　　　　　　　　_____　　_____

2. a large area of land　　　　　　　　_____　　_____

3. happening every year　　　　　　　_____　　_____

4. made into liquid by heat　　　　　　_____　　_____

5. extremely difficult to live in　　　　_____　　_____

6. to make or create something　　　　_____　　_____

7. from the beginning of the year to the end　_____　　_____

8. a body of rock or gas that goes around a star in space　_____　　_____

B Write the correct words or phrases to complete the sentences.

harsh	poisonous	always	each year

1. I have _____ dreamed of going to Spain.

2. El Niño could cause a _____ winter in Europe.

3. Many people try to climb the mountain _____.

4. Make sure you don't touch these _____ mushrooms.

Writing Practice

A Unscramble the words to complete the sentences.

1. (a living / way / to / a / difficult / make)
   ➤ It's _____.

2. (for / are / live in / impossible / anything / to)
   ➤ These lakes _____.

3. (heard / of / you / Ethiopia / ever / the region of Dallol / in)
   ➤ Have _____?

4. (unlivable / one / on / places / the most / of / the planet)
   ➤ It is _____.

5. (because of / the potash mines / conditions / gave up / harsh / the)
   ➤ They _____.

B Translate the sentences into your language, focusing on the meanings of the underlined parts.

1. Dallol has <u>the highest</u> average annual temperature on Earth.
   ➤ _____

2. Americans discovered an important mineral there <u>in the late 1910s</u>.
   ➤ _____

3. People ride camels <u>to get</u> there and use axes <u>to chop</u> big pieces of salt from the ground.
   ➤ _____

Unit 8 Andy Goldsworthy, a Unique Artist

Vocabulary Practice

A Write each word next to its correct definition. Then write its meaning in your language.

| spiral | freeze | icicle | sculpture |
| smash | patience | swirl | appreciate |

1. a twisting movement _____ _____
2. circling around a central point _____ _____
3. to become hard because of ice _____ _____
4. to hit two objects together with force _____ _____
5. the ability to wait a long time for something _____ _____
6. to enjoy something because you understand it _____ _____
7. a hanging piece of ice made from dripping water _____ _____
8. a piece of art made from rock, wood, or other solid material _____ _____

B Write the correct words to complete the sentences.

| broke | enjoy | tolerance | freezes |

1. Water _____ to form ice.
2. I have no _____ for any kind of violence.
3. He _____ the car window to save his dog.
4. Let's get out there and _____ ourselves, everyone.

16

Writing Practice

A Unscramble the words to complete the sentences.

1. (is / easy / to / Andy's / not / art / make)

   ▶ _____.

2. (to make / use / doesn't / his art / paints)

   ▶ He _____.

3. (uses / the powder / to turn / water / into paint)

   ▶ He _____.

4. (with / beautiful / makes / sculptures / ice / he)

   ▶ _____.

5. (part of / other / Andy's art / natural objects / become)

   ▶ Many _____.

B Translate the sentences into your language, focusing on the meanings of the underlined parts.

1. Andy holds the icicles together <u>until</u> they <u>freeze into</u> a large piece.

   ▶ _____

2. He also smashes rocks together <u>to get colored powder</u> from them.

   ▶ _____

3. That <u>makes</u> Andy's art something <u>that</u> everyone can appreciate and enjoy.

   ▶ _____

Unit 8 17

Unit 9 City, Town, Village

Vocabulary Practice

A Write each word next to its correct definition. Then write its meaning in your language.

| mayor | council | document | somewhere |
| legal | collection | community | incorporated |

1. related with the law _____ _____
2. having a legal status _____ _____
3. a group of objects or people _____ _____
4. the elected head of a city _____ _____
5. a group of people living in the same place _____ _____
6. a group of elected people who manage a city _____ _____
7. in or at a place that you do not know or do not mention by name _____ _____
8. an official paper or book that gives information about something _____ _____

B Write the correct words to complete the sentences.

| collection | accident | regional | governmental |

1. It was an _____. It wasn't supposed to happen.
2. The _____ competition takes place in February.
3. There was a large _____ of books in the apartment.
4. The city is the economic and _____ center of Denmark.

Writing Practice

A Unscramble the words to complete the sentences.

1. (between / clearer / them / difference)

   ➤ There is a _____.

2. (few / has / small / and / people)

   ➤ A village is _____.

3. (is / the / somewhere / a town / middle / in)

   ➤ _____.

4. (do / have / power / any / not / villages / governmental)

   ➤ Towns and _____.

5. (families / of / usually / a small / farming / collection)

   ➤ A village is _____.

B Translate the sentences into your language, focusing on the meanings of the underlined parts.

1. It says that the community is a city, not a town.

   ➤ _____

2. It can be difficult to know the difference between a city, a town, and a village.

   ➤ _____

3. A village doesn't have department stores, which a city or a town may have.

   ➤ _____

Unit 10: Starbucks of the 18th Century

Vocabulary Practice

A Write each word or phrase next to its correct definition. Then write its meaning in your language.

relax	public	politics	educated
dress up	share	sneak	composer

1. to move quietly _____ _____
2. having an education _____ _____
3. activities of government _____ _____
4. to rest and enjoy yourself _____ _____
5. a person who writes music _____ _____
6. to tell someone about your feelings, ideas, etc. _____ _____
7. able to be used by anyone; not private _____ _____
8. to wear special clothes to pretend to be somebody else _____ _____

B Write the correct words or phrases to complete the sentences.

social	pleasure	educated	take it easy

1. _____ and you'll be fine.
2. It is a _____ working with you.
3. She isn't _____ enough to understand what I mean.
4. The high cost of college has become a _____ problem.

Writing Practice

A Unscramble the words to complete the sentences.

1. (to / went / coffeehouses / talk / to)
   ▶ Educated men _____.

2. (social media / and ideas / to / information / share)
   ▶ We use _____.

3. (to / the men / go to / coffeehouses / with / allowed)
   ▶ Women were not _____.

4. (talk / to / of the day / about / went there / the news)
   ▶ Men often _____.

5. (in / there / none of / were / those things / century / the 18th)
   ▶ _____.

B Translate the sentences into your language, focusing on the meanings of the underlined parts.

1. Coffeehouses <u>were filled with</u> exciting talks about life and politics.
   ▶ _____

2. Nowadays, coffeehouses are just places <u>to relax</u> with a cup of coffee.
   ▶ _____

3. It can be difficult <u>for us</u> <u>to imagine</u> how exciting coffeehouses <u>used to</u> be.
   ▶ _____

Unit 11 Why Trees Matter

Vocabulary Practice

A Write each word next to its correct definition. Then write its meaning in your language.

| pollution | moist | shade | essential |
| ecosystem | benefit | mature | ecologist |

1. slightly wet _____ _____

2. a good or helpful result _____ _____

3. fully grown and developed _____ _____

4. very important and necessary _____ _____

5. the action of making the land, water, and air dirty _____ _____

6. an area of darkness made when something blocks the sun _____ _____

7. a scientist who studies living things and the environment _____ _____

8. all the living and non-living things in an environment _____ _____

B Write the correct words to complete the sentences.

| novelist | psychologist | ecologist | mature |

1. She is a wildlife _____ and snake expert.

2. The Chinese _____ wrote a book about their friendship.

3. The tree is _____ enough to produce a good amount of fruit.

4. It will be helpful to consult a _____ during times of stress.

22

Writing Practice

A **Unscramble the words to complete the sentences.**

1. (are / trees / home / ecosystems / to / complex)
   ➤ Mature _____.

2. (for / essential / of / the health / the environment)
   ➤ Trees are _____.

3. (can / species / live in / tree / different / a single)
   ➤ Up to 500 _____!

4. (to / talk / going / the importance / about / for our world / of trees)
   ➤ We are _____.

5. (I / trees / didn't / so much / affect / realize / the environment)
   ➤ _____.

B **Translate the sentences into your language, focusing on the meanings of the underlined parts.**

1. This can reduce air conditioner usage <u>by</u> <u>as much as</u> 30 percent.
   ➤ _____

2. <u>Having beautiful trees</u> increases the value of a home <u>between</u> 5 <u>and</u> 18 percent.
   ➤ _____

3. My research has found <u>that</u> trees reduce the temperature in cities <u>by up to</u> 7 degrees Celsius.
   ➤ _____

Unit 12 Penny Harvest

Vocabulary Practice

A Write each word or phrase next to its correct definition. Then write its meaning in your language.

harvest	raise	stray	so far
immigrant	phase	involve	penny

1. until the present time _____ _____

2. a coin or a unit of money _____ _____

3. not having a home, or lost _____ _____

4. a stage or part of a process _____ _____

5. to bring or collect money together _____ _____

6. to cause someone to take part in something _____ _____

7. a time when crops are gathered from the fields _____ _____

8. a person who comes to another country to live _____ _____

B Write the correct words to complete the sentences.

happen	involve	collect	homeless

1. I'm sorry to hear that. When did it _____?

2. There are many _____ people in the street.

3. We want to _____ a lot of money to help poor people.

4. The teacher tried to _____ all her students in the game.

Writing Practice

A   Unscramble the words to complete the sentences.

1. (the house / have / pennies / around / a lot of)

   ▶ People _____.

2. (more / become / in / involved / the community)

   ▶ The students _____.

3. (to / bring / a group of / back / student leaders / these pennies)

   ▶ The students _____.

4. (to / and planted / immigrants / English / gardens / the community / in)

   ▶ Students have taught _____.

5. (how / for / students / a program / teaching / to / in their communities / help out)

   ▶ A Penny Harvest is _____.

B   Translate the sentences into your language, focusing on the meanings of the underlined parts.

1. These activities <u>help the students learn</u> more about their communities.

   ▶ _____

2. The student leaders decide <u>what</u> they <u>want to do</u> with the money.

   ▶ _____

3. Students go to their neighbors' houses with their parents <u>and collect pennies</u>.

   ▶ _____

Tips for Saving Time

Vocabulary Practice

A Write each word or phrase next to its correct definition. Then write its meaning in your language.

relief	fantastic	distraction	efficiently
task	challenging	concentrate	keep track of

1. very good _____ _____

2. a job for someone to do _____ _____

3. to watch or follow the process of _____ _____

4. to give all your attention to something _____ _____

5. done without wasting time or energy _____ _____

6. difficult in a way that is usually interesting _____ _____

7. a pleasant feeling after something stressful stops _____ _____

8. something that makes it difficult to think or pay attention _____ _____

B Write the correct words to complete the sentences.

proudly	challenging	beautifully	dangerously

1. She played the piano so _____.

2. The job is exciting but really _____.

3. My sister _____ showed off her trophy.

4. He is driving the bus very _____. He needs to slow down!

26

Writing Practice

A **Unscramble the words to complete the sentences.**

1. (feel / after / them / finishing / relief)
   ➤ You'll _____.

2. (tips / done / time saving / more work / to get)
   ➤ Follow these _____.

3. (time / spend / won't / doing / too much / any one activity)
   ➤ You _____.

4. (possible / more / use / to / efficiently / your time)
   ➤ It is _____.

5. (helps / your time / a schedule / you / keep track of)
   ➤ _____.

B **Translate the sentences into your language, focusing on the meanings of the underlined parts.**

1. Write down <u>the activities you want to do</u> each day.
   ➤ _____

2. Most people are <u>too</u> tired <u>to</u> do these difficult jobs late in the day.
   ➤ _____

3. <u>When</u> you <u>have to concentrate on</u> a task, turn off the Internet.
   ➤ _____

Unit 14: The Amber Room

Vocabulary Practice

A Write each word or phrase next to its correct definition. Then write its meaning in your language.

| decorate | amaze | take over | ship |
| precious | royal | take apart | exist |

1. to be real _____ _____
2. very valuable _____ _____
3. to surprise greatly _____ _____
4. to take control of something _____ _____
5. a member of the family of a king or queen _____ _____
6. to remove or separate the parts of something _____ _____
7. to send something by ship or by another means of transport _____ _____
8. to make something look better by putting other things on it _____ _____

B Write the correct words to complete the sentences.

| adorned | valuable | surprised | apart |

1. The bad news _____ all of us.
2. He had to take the engine _____ to fix it.
3. The most _____ thing in life is friendship.
4. The dining table was _____ with beautiful flowers.

28

Writing Practice

A Unscramble the words to complete the sentences.

1. (as / the room / to think / used / a place)

    ➤ Some _____.

2. (to / what / knows / nobody / it / happened)

    ➤ _____.

3. (for / used / royals / the room / things / different)

    ➤ Russian _____.

4. (a lot of / the Amber Room / decorate / to / amber)

    ➤ Builders used _____.

5. (was / the room / believe / 1944 / destroyed / in)

    ➤ Most historians _____.

B Translate the sentences into your language, focusing on the meanings of the underlined parts.

1. Russian officials <u>tried to</u> move the room but they <u>couldn't</u>.

    ➤ _____

2. The Amber Room was a beautiful, expensive room <u>built in Prussia</u> in the early 18th century.

    ➤ _____

3. This theory got special attention <u>when</u> a piece from the Amber Room <u>was found</u> in 1997 in Germany.

    ➤ _____

Unit 15 Where Did the Moon Come from?

Vocabulary Practice

A Write each word next to its correct definition. Then write its meaning in your language.

| theory | claim | crash | gravity |
| collision | origin | capture | physicist |

1. to take and hold something　　　　　　_____　_____
2. the point where something begins　　　_____　_____
3. to hit something else very hard　　　　_____　_____
4. a scientific explanation for something　_____　_____
5. an accident where two objects hit each other　_____　_____
6. the force that causes things to fall towards the Earth　_____　_____
7. a scientist who studies nature and how objects move　_____　_____
8. to say something is true when some people say it is not true　_____　_____

B Write the correct words to complete the sentences.

| catch | hit | claimed | origin |

1. We set traps to _____ the mice.
2. The _____ of this word is unknown.
3. The ball _____ the window and broke the glass.
4. They _____ that their product is made from natural ingredients.

Writing Practice

A Unscramble the words to complete the sentences.

1. (us / where / tell / came / the moon / from)
   ➤ Can you _____?

2. (the pieces of / formed / rock / behind / from / left)
   ➤ The moon _____.

3. (several / are / the origin / the moon / about / of / theories)
   ➤ There _____.

4. (the moon / in / elsewhere / formed / that / the solar system)
   ➤ Another idea is _____.

5. (years ago / the Earth / crashed / into / about / 4.5 billion)
   ➤ Another planet _____.

B Translate the sentences into your language, focusing on the meanings of the underlined parts.

1. People think the moon is <u>a lot closer than</u> it really is.
   ➤ _____

2. The moon came <u>close enough</u> for Earth's gravity <u>to</u> capture it.
   ➤ _____

3. Another theory claims <u>that</u> the Earth and the moon were actually formed <u>at the same time</u>.
   ➤ _____

Unit 15

Unit 16 The Mysterious Box on Airplanes

Vocabulary Practice

A Write each word next to its correct definition. Then write its meaning in your language.

locate	copilot	spot	search
flight	damage	crash	cockpit

1. to see; to notice _____ _____
2. to put in a particular place _____ _____
3. to carefully look for something _____ _____
4. the place where pilots or drivers sits _____ _____
5. the airplane that is making a journey _____ _____
6. physical harm that is done to something _____ _____
7. the person who helps the pilot fly the plane _____ _____
8. an accident where a plane or a car is seriously damaged _____ _____

B Write the correct words or phrases to complete the sentences.

collision	notice	flight	looked for

1. I didn't _____ her leaving early.
2. What time is your _____ to New York?
3. I _____ my cat for two hours before finally finding her.
4. Eight people were injured in a _____ between two trains.

Writing Practice

A **Unscramble the words to complete the sentences.**

1. (is / bright / color / orange / in / the black box)

    ▶ _____.

2. (in / is / the tail / of / located / the plane)

    ▶ The black box _____.

3. (is / know / the black box / that / important)

    ▶ Most people _____.

4. (ever / about / a news report / heard / an airplane crash)

    ▶ Have you _____?

5. (know / does / about / the black box / what / don't)

    ▶ They _____.

B **Translate the sentences into your language, focusing on the meanings of the underlined parts.**

1. In a crash, the tail usually receives <u>the smallest</u> amount of damage.

    ▶ _____

2. The black box records everything <u>that happens in the cockpit</u> during a flight.

    ▶ _____

3. This makes it very easy <u>to</u> spot <u>when</u> officials <u>are searching</u> the ground or ocean <u>for</u> it.

    ▶ _____

Unit 17 Wasps Help Protect Corn

Vocabulary Practice

A Write each word next to its correct definition. Then write its meaning in your language.

| wasp | defense | entire | sting |
| protect | fascinating | chemical | cloud |

1. all; complete _____ _____
2. very interesting _____ _____
3. to keep from harm _____ _____
4. a way to stop something from attacking _____ _____
5. a substance that produced by a chemical process _____ _____
6. a black-and-yellow flying insect that can sting _____ _____
7. to cause pain with a sharp part that usually has poison _____ _____
8. a large amount of something in the air such as smoke or dust _____ _____

B Write the correct words to complete the sentences.

| chemicals | protection | whole | interesting |

1. I was sick for a _____ week.
2. They had no _____ from the government.
3. The novel was so _____ that I couldn't stop reading it.
4. These two _____ make the color of the candy change.

34

Writing Practice

A **Unscramble the words to complete the sentences.**

1. (very / wasps / are / in / important / nature)
   ➤ _____.

2. (protect / help / being / corn / to / from / eaten)
   ➤ Wasps _____.

3. (an / defense system / these hungry bugs / amazing / against)
   ➤ Corn has _____.

4. (what / is / the corn / kind of bug / eating / the wasp / tell)
   ➤ The chemicals _____.

5. (for / a / food / and worms / small insects / popular / many)
   ➤ Corn is _____.

B **Translate the sentences into your language, focusing on the meanings of the underlined parts.**

1. <u>Without</u> these wasps, the worms <u>would</u> eat the entire crop of corn.
   ➤ _____

2. The plant sends out <u>a cloud of</u> these chemicals<u>, which</u> have a special smell.
   ➤ _____

3. <u>If</u> a different kind of worm <u>is eating</u> it, the corn can <u>send out</u> a different chemical.
   ➤ _____

Unit 18 Weird Sports

Vocabulary Practice

A Write each word next to its correct definition. Then write its meaning in your language.

| obstacle | hold | predictable | slippery |
| originate | course | participant | competition |

1. to be produced or created _____ _____
2. a path or track used during a race _____ _____
3. to have a meeting, competition, etc. _____ _____
4. a person who is taking part in an event _____ _____
5. able to be guessed or known ahead of time _____ _____
6. a fight or rivalry between two or more people _____ _____
7. something that makes it difficult to continue _____ _____
8. difficult to stand on because of water, ice, or oil _____ _____

B Write the correct words to complete the sentences.

| contest | barriers | expected | participants |

1. Oil prices are _____ to rise this year.
2. There were many _____ in the workshop.
3. We had to stand far behind the _____ to be safe.
4. The school is having a Halloween party and costume _____.

Writing Practice

A   Unscramble the words to complete the sentences.

1. (was / in Turkey / first competition / held)
   ▶ The _____.

2. (an / in / sport / 1992 / official / became)
   ▶ It _____.

3. (finish / is / the course / the winner / fastest)
   ▶ The man to _____.

4. (can / a sport / you / play / that / your wife / with)
   ▶ Do you want _____?

5. (try / to the ground / players / wrestle / the other / to)
   ▶ They _____.

B   Translate the sentences into your language, focusing on the meanings of the underlined parts.

1. A man <u>must</u> carry a woman through a course <u>as fast as possible</u>.
   ▶ _____

2. Participants cover their bodies in olive oil <u>to make</u> themselves slippery.
   ▶ _____

3. If regular wrestling is not <u>challenging enough</u> for you, then you <u>should try</u> oil wrestling.
   ▶ _____

Unit 18   37

Unit 19 The Future of Travel

Vocabulary Practice

A Write each word or phrase next to its correct definition. Then write its meaning in your language.

| aircraft | decade | reality | magnetic |
| currently | passenger | improve | come up with |

1. to make better _____ _____
2. now; at this time _____ _____
3. a period of ten years _____ _____
4. a vehicle that flies in the air _____ _____
5. a person who rides in a vehicle _____ _____
6. able to attract with electric charge _____ _____
7. something the actually exists or happens _____ _____
8. to think of an idea or solution to a problem _____ _____

B Write the correct words or phrases to complete the sentences.

| reality | develop | at present | produce |

1. I'm trying to _____ new music.
2. Take this course to _____ your drawing skills.
3. _____, my mom is working as an English teacher.
4. His dream of becoming a pilot became a _____.

Writing Practice

A Unscramble the words to complete the sentences.

1. (would / these cars / driven / computers / by / be)
   ➤ _____.

2. (to / improve / want / the future / for / transportation)
   ➤ They _____.

3. (seems / happen / like / will / it / that dream / never)
   ➤ Nowadays _____.

4. (changes / a light aircraft / into a car / that / designing)
   ➤ Engineers are _____.

5. (the city / able to / an hour / move around / at 240 kilometers)
   ➤ People will be _____.

B Translate the sentences into your language, focusing on the meanings of the underlined parts.

1. It <u>may</u> be a long time <u>before</u> flying cars are a reality.
   ➤ _____

2. People believed <u>that</u> someday we <u>would</u> drive in flying cars.
   ➤ _____

3. Scientists have a lot of ideas about <u>how to</u> <u>make</u> future travel <u>faster and safer</u>.
   ➤ _____

Unit 19 39

Unit 20: The Power of a Dream

Vocabulary Practice

A Write each word next to its correct definition. Then write its meaning in your language.

| paddle | explore | journey | arrest |
| achieve | exotic | encourage | pursue |

1. a long trip _____ _____
2. to move a boat with an oar _____ _____
3. to reach a goal by working hard _____ _____
4. very different, strange, or unusual _____ _____
5. to travel around a country to learn about it _____ _____
6. to try to get something over a period of time _____ _____
7. to make someone more likely to do something _____ _____
8. to take a person away and keep the person at a police station _____ _____

B Write the correct words to complete the sentences.

| explore | accomplished | inspired | pursue |

1. I feel proud that I _____ my goal.
2. We'll continue to _____ that mission.
3. He _____ me to write this book.
4. There are many great places to _____ in the area.

Writing Practice

A Unscramble the words to complete the sentences.

1. (was / in England / Jason / born / in 1967)
   ► _____.

2. (students / encouraged / their / pursue / to / dreams)
   ► He _____.

3. (became / in / he / traveling / interested / in 1985)
   ► _____.

4. (want / made / exotic / to / other / lands / him / explore)
   ► His trip _____.

5. (to / dream / the world / only his muscles / travel around / using)
   ► Jason Lewis had a _____.

B Translate the sentences into your language, focusing on the meanings of the underlined parts.

1. It took nine months <u>for him</u> <u>to heal and get back</u> on the road again.
   ► _____

2. He <u>was arrested</u> because the Egyptian police thought he was a spy.
   ► _____

3. <u>Even if</u> it is very difficult or takes a long time, <u>try to</u> achieve your dream.
   ► _____

Unit 20 41

Reading Voyage 1
BASIC

Scan this QR Code for MP3 files

Reading Voyage is an eleven-level reading series divided into four stages: Starter, Basic, Plus, and Expert. The series is designed for high-beginner to low-advanced EFL students who want to enhance their reading abilities. The passages cover a wide range of topics that enable learners to expand their background knowledge. The various exercises will allow students to develop their reading comprehension, critical thinking, and vocabulary skills.

Key Features

- Appealing and informative texts covering a variety of topics
- Comprehension questions to help identify main ideas and details
- Reading Skill and Summary to help students analyze key concepts
- Vocabulary Expansion presenting synonyms, prefixes, and more
- Workbook for additional vocabulary and writing practice

Components

Student Book / Workbook

Download Resources at www.darakwon.co.kr:

MP3 files / Answer Key / Translations / Vocabulary lists

Reading Voyage Series: BASIC

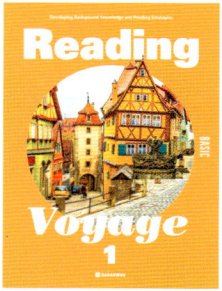  

170-200 words   200-230 words   230-260 words